What People Are Saying About Threshold Bible Study

"This remarkable series provides a method of study and reflection that is bound to produce rich fruit." Dianne Bergant, C.S.A., Catholic Theological Union, Chicago

"This fine series will provide needed tools that can deepen your understanding of Scripture, but most importantly it can deepen your faith." Most Reverend Charles J. Chaput, O.F.M. Cap., Archbishop of Denver

"Threshold Bible Study is a wonderful series that helps modern people read the Bible with insight and joy." Richard J. Clifford, S.J., Weston Jesuit School of Theology

"The commentary of Stephen Binz does far more than inform; it asks for commitment and assent on the part of the reader/prayer." Kathleen O'Connell Chesto, author of *F.I.R.E.* and *Why Are the Dandelions Weeds?*

"This is a wonderful gift for those wishing to make a home for the Word in their hearts." Carol J. Dempsey, OP, Associate Professor of Theology, University of Portland, OR

"Written in a sprightly easy-to-understand style, these volumes will engage the mind, heart, and spirit." Alexander A. Di Lella, O.F.M., The Catholic University of America

"By covering a wide variety of themes and topics, Threshold Bible Study continually breathes new life into ancient texts." John R. Donahue, S.J., St. Mary's Seminary and University

"Threshold Bible Study successfully bridges the painful gap between solid biblical scholarship and the rich spiritual nourishment that we expect to find in the words of Scripture." Demetrius Dumm, O.S.B., Saint Vincent Archabbey

"Threshold Bible Study offers a marvelous new approach for individuals and groups to study themes in our rich biblical and theological tradition." John Endres, S.J., Jesuit School of Theology, Berkeley

"Threshold Bible Study enables Catholics to read, with greater understanding, the Bible in the Church." Francis Cardinal George, O.M.I., Archbishop of Chicago

"Threshold Bible Study offers you an encounter with the Word that will make your heart come alive." Tim Gray, Director of the Denver Catholic Biblical School

"Threshold Bible Study offers solid scholarship and spiritual depth."
Scott Hahn, Franciscan University of Steubenville

"Threshold Bible Study offers those who want to begin faith-filled and prayerful study of the Bible with a user-friendly tool."   Leslie J. Hoppe, O.F.M., Catholic Theological Union

"Threshold Bible Study is a fine blend of the best of biblical scholarship and a realistic sensitivity to the spiritual journey of the believing Christian."
Francis J. Moloney, S.D.B., The Catholic University of America

"An invaluable guide that can make reading the Bible enjoyable and truly nourishing."
Jacques Nieuviarts, Institut Catholique de Toulouse

"Threshold Bible Study is a refreshing approach to enable participants to ponder the Scriptures more deeply."   Irene Nowell, O.S.B., Mount St. Scholastica

"Threshold Bible Study stands in the tradition of the biblical renewal movement and brings it back to life."   Kathleen M. O'Connor, Columbia Theological Seminary

"This series is exceptional for its scholarly solidity, pastoral practicality, and clarity of presentation."   Peter C. Phan, Georgetown University

"Threshold Bible Study is the perfect series of Bible study books for serious students with limited time."   John J. Pilch, Georgetown University

"These thematic books are informative, easy to use, rooted in the Church's tradition of reflection and prayer, and of sound catechetical method."
Most Reverend Anthony M. Pilla, Bishop of Cleveland

"Threshold Bible Study is an enriching and enlightening approach to understanding the rich faith which the Scriptures hold for us today."
Abbot Gregory J. Polan, O.S.B., Conception Abbey and Seminary College

"Threshold Bible Study leads the reader from Bible study to personal prayer, community involvement, and active Christian commitment in the world."
Sandra M. Schneiders, Jesuit School of Theology, Berkeley

"This is the best material I have seen for serious Bible study."
Most Reverend Donald W. Trautman, Bishop of Erie

"Guaranteed to make your love of Scripture grow!"
Ronald D. Witherup, S.S., author of The Bible Companion

MYSTERIES
of the ROSARY

Stephen J. Binz

TWENTY
THIRD 23rd
PUBLICATIONS

Third Printing 2013

The Scripture passages contained herein are from the *New Revised Standard Version of the Bible*, Catholic edition. Copyright ©1989, by the Division of Christian Education of the National Council of Churches in the U.S.A. All rights reserved.

TWENTY-THIRD PUBLICATIONS
A Division of Bayard
One Montauk Avenue, Suite 200
New London, CT 06320
(860) 437-3012 or (800) 321-0411
www.23rdpublications.com
ISBN 978-1-58595-519-0

Library of Congress Catalog Card Number: 2005929306
Printed in the U.S.A.

Contents

LESSONS 13–18

LESSONS 19–24

LESSONS 25–30

How to Use Threshold Bible Study

Each book in the Threshold Bible Study series is designed to lead you through a new doorway of biblical awareness, to accompany you across a unique threshold of understanding. The characters, places, and images that you encounter in each of these topical studies will help you explore fresh dimensions of your faith and discover richer insights for your spiritual life.

Threshold Bible Study covers biblical themes in depth in a short amount of time. Unlike more traditional Bible studies that treat a biblical book or series of books, Threshold Bible Study aims to address specific topics within the entire Bible. The goal is not for you to comprehend everything about each passage, but rather for you to understand what a variety of passages from different books of the Bible reveals about the topic of each study.

Threshold Bible Study offers you an opportunity to explore the entire Bible from the viewpoint of a variety of different themes. The commentary that follows each biblical passage launches your reflection about that passage and helps you begin to see its significance within the context of your contemporary experience. The questions following the commentary challenge you to understand the passage more fully and apply it to your own life. The prayer starter helps conclude your study by integrating learning into your relationship with God.

These studies are designed for maximum flexibility. Each study is presented in a workbook format, with sections for reading, reflecting, writing, discussing, and praying. Space for writing after each question is ideal for personal study and allows group members to prepare in advance for their discussion. The thirty lessons in each topic may be used by an individual over the period of a month, or by a group for six sessions, with lessons to be studied each week before the next group meeting. These studies are ideal for Bible study groups, small Christian communities, adult faith formation, student groups, Sunday school, neighborhood groups, and family reading, as well as for individual learning.

The method of Threshold Bible Study is rooted in the classical tradition of *lectio divina*, an ancient yet contemporary means for reading the Scriptures reflectively and prayerfully. Reading and interpreting the text (*lectio*) is followed by reflective meditation on its message (*meditatio*). This reading and reflecting flows into prayer from the heart (*oratio* and *contemplatio*).

This ancient method assures us that Bible study is a matter of both the mind and the heart. It is not just an intellectual exercise to learn more and be able to discuss the Bible with others. It is, more importantly, a transforming experience. Reflecting on God's word, guided by the Holy Spirit, illumines the mind with wisdom and stirs the heart with zeal.

Following the personal Bible study, Threshold Bible Study offers a method for extending lectio divina into a weekly conversation with a small group. This communal experience will allow participants to enhance their appreciation of the message and build up a spiritual community (*collatio*). The end result will be to increase not only individual faith, but also faithful witness in the context of daily life (*operatio*).

Through the spiritual disciplines of Scripture reading, study, reflection, conversation, and prayer, you will experience God's grace more abundantly as your life is rooted more deeply in Christ. The risen Jesus said: "Listen! I am standing at the door, knocking; if you hear my voice and open the door, I will come in to you and eat with you, and you with me" (Rev 3:20). Listen to the Word of God, open the door, and cross the threshold to an unimaginable dwelling with God!

SUGGESTIONS FOR INDIVIDUAL STUDY

• Make your Bible reading a time of prayer. Ask for God's guidance as your read the Scriptures.

• Try to study daily, or as often as possible according to the circumstances of your life.

• Read the Bible passage carefully, trying to understand both its meaning and its personal application as you read. Some persons find it helpful to read the passage aloud.

• Read the passage in another Bible translation. Each version adds to your understanding of the original text.

• Allow the commentary to help you comprehend and apply the scriptural text. The commentary is only a beginning, not the last word on the meaning of the passage.

• After reflecting on each question, write out your responses. The very act of writing will help you clarify your thoughts, bring new insights, and amplify your understanding.

• As you reflect on your answers, think about how you can live God's word in the context of your daily life.

• Conclude each daily lesson by reading the prayer and continuing with your own prayer from the heart.

• Make sure your reflections and prayers are matters of both the mind and the heart. A true encounter with God's word is always a transforming experience.

• Choose a word or a phrase from the lesson to carry with you throughout the day as a reminder of your encounter with God's life-changing word.

• Share your learning experience with at least one other person whom you trust for additional insights and affirmation. The ideal way to share learning is in a small group that meets regularly.

SUGGESTIONS FOR GROUP STUDY

• Meet regularly; weekly is ideal. Try to be on time and make attendance a high priority for the sake of the group. The average group meets for about an hour.

• Open each session with a prepared prayer, a song, or a reflection. Find some appropriate way to bring the group from the workaday world into a sacred time of graced sharing.

• If you have not been together before, name tags are very helpful as a group begins to become acquainted with the other group members.

• Spend the first session getting acquainted with one another, reading the Introduction aloud, and discussing the questions that follow.

• Appoint a group facilitator to provide guidance to the discussion. The role of facilitator may rotate among members each week. The facilitator simply keeps the discussion on track; each person shares responsibility for the group. There is no need for the facilitator to be a trained teacher.

• Try to study the six lessons on your own during the week. When you have done your own reflection and written your own answers, you will be better prepared to discuss the six scriptural lessons with the group. If you have not had an opportunity to study the passages during the week, meet with the group anyway to share support and insights.

• Participate in the discussion as much as you are able, offering your thoughts, insights, feelings, and decisions. You learn by sharing with others the fruits of your study.

• Be careful not to dominate the discussion. It is important that everyone in the group be offered an equal opportunity to share the results of their work. Try to link what you say to the comments of others so that the group remains on the topic.

• When discussing your own personal thoughts or feelings, use "I" language. Be as personal and honest as appropriate and be very cautious about giving advice to others.

• Listen attentively to the other members of the group so as to learn from their insights. The words of the Bible affect each person in a different way, so a group provides a wealth of understanding for each member.

• Don't fear silence. Silence in a group is as important as silence in personal study. It allows individuals time to listen to the voice of God's Spirit and the opportunity to form their thoughts before they speak.

• Solicit several responses for each question. The thoughts of different people will build on the answers of others and will lead to deeper insights for all.

• Don't fear controversy. Differences of opinions are a sign of a healthy and honest group. If you cannot resolve an issue, continue on, agreeing to disagree. There is probably some truth in each viewpoint.

• Discuss the questions that seem most important for the group. There is no need to cover all the questions in the group session.

• Realize that some questions about the Bible cannot be resolved, even by experts. Don't get stuck on some issue for which there are no clear answers.

• Whatever is said in the group is said in confidence and should be regarded as such.

• Pray as a group in whatever way feels comfortable. Pray for the members of your group throughout the week.

Schedule for group study

Session 1: Introduction   Date: _____

Session 2: Lessons 1-6   Date: _____

Session 3: Lessons 7-12   Date: _____

Session 4: Lessons 13-18   Date: _____

Session 5: Lessons 19-24   Date: _____

Session 6: Lessons 25-30   Date: _____

Mary treasured all these words and pondered them in her heart. Luke 2:19

The Mysteries of the Rosary

Imagine looking upon the face of Jesus through the eyes of Mary. Imagine pondering the words and deeds of Jesus with Mary's mind. Imagine feeling the joys and sufferings of Jesus with Mary's heart. This is the type of imaginative meditation to which the rosary invites us. The rosary is a reflective prayer that we offer to God in union with Mary.

In Christian tradition, Mary is honored primarily for two reasons: she is the mother of Christ and she is the model of discipleship. The gospel of Luke expresses this double honor. First, the gospel reveres Mary as the bearer of Christ: "Blessed are you among women, and blessed is the fruit of your womb" (Luke 1:42). She is the human instrument through which God would bring the Messiah into the world, the vessel through which divinity would join with humanity in her Son. Second, the gospel honors her as an ideal disciple: "Blessed is she who believed that there would be a fulfillment of what was spoken to her by the Lord" (Luke 1:45). She listens to God's word and she trusts that God would bring about the salvation that he promised.

Mary was with Jesus from the moment of his conception. As his mother, she gave him life and shared her human likeness with him. She taught him the Scriptures of Israel and the traditions of their people. With Joseph her husband, she brought Jesus to the temple in Jerusalem to celebrate the feasts of Judaism and taught him to sing the psalms. After narrating the events of

Jesus' childhood, the gospel says, "She treasured all these things and pondered them in her heart" (Luke 2:19, 51).

Mary remained intimately united with Jesus through his adult ministry. John's gospel tells us that she was with Jesus at his first public miracle at Cana (John 2:1–5). She remained with Jesus all the way to his cross as she watched him suffer and die (John 19:25–27). The Acts of the Apostles tells us that she was part of the community of disciples that remained in Jerusalem after Christ's resurrection and ascension and that experienced the coming of the Holy Spirit (Acts 1:14). No one knows Jesus better than Mary, and no one can help us understand the mysteries of his saving life better than Mary.

When praying the rosary, the focus of our attention is Christ and his saving life. Yet, we ask Mary for her prayerful support and guidance, that we may walk in faith as she did. We want to entrust our lives to God like her, praying with her, "Let it be, thy will be done." And so we honor Mary along with Christians down through the ages who have expressed admiration and affection for her through feasts, paintings, music, and devotional practices. When we give honor to Mary, we are praising the great things that God has accomplished in her. God took the fragile human life of Mary of Nazareth and transformed her life with his grace into humanity's exemplar. She is the radiant daughter of the Father, tender mother of the Son, and beloved spouse of the Holy Spirit. Through God's grace she is united most fully with the life of God and she shows us the way to an intimate, interior union with God.

Reflection and discussion

• What are my previous experiences of praying the rosary? Which experiences of prayer do I remember best?

• Why do we meditate on the mysteries of the rosary in union with the prayers of Mary?

An Ancient and Evolving Tradition of Meditation

Nearly every ancient religion of the world has a tradition of using prayer beads as a devotional tool for meditation. Primitive forms of prayer beads were made of fruit seeds, dried berries, pieces of bone, shells, and hardened clay. More affluent devotees used strings of coral, precious stones, pearls, and jewels. The Hindu and Buddhist prayer beads predate Christianity, and there are normally 108 beads on the string. Repeating a mantra on each bead drives away evil and fills the person praying with peace and bliss. The prayer beads of Islam consist of 99 beads, or often 33 beads repeated three times, on which each of the names or attributes of Allah are recited.

The development of the present-day rosary of the Christian tradition has roots in the distant past. The desert monks of the fourth century developed a system for counting prayers using a circular string of knotted wool. The cord could be used for counting any kind of prayer or devotional exercise, but typically the Jesus Prayer: "Lord, Jesus Christ, Son of God, have mercy on me." The prayer was chanted slowly as the one praying inhaled and exhaled. By the eleventh century, the custom of praying 150 Our Fathers in place of the 150 psalms chanted in the monasteries was widespread among the laity. It became common practice for lay people to carry a "Paternoster cord" of 50 knots or beads, to be repeated three times. Soon thereafter, as popular devotion to Mary increased, the joys of Mary were recounted by praying antiphons to Mary on a similar circlet of beads. Most common among these prayers were the greeting of the angel Gabriel, "Hail Mary, full of grace, the Lord is with thee," and the greeting of Elizabeth, "Blessed art thou among women and blessed is the fruit of thy womb." In thirteenth century London and Paris, crafting strings of Paternoster and Ave beads became a specialized industry with its own guilds of artisans.

In a parallel development, chains of 150 phrases from the lives of Jesus and Mary, extending from the Annunciation to their glorification in heaven, were commonly prayed in popular devotions. In the fifteenth century, these phrases were joined to the Hail Mary prayers and the devotion began to be called a *rosarium*, a rose garden. So long as the rosary consisted of 150 meditative phrases, it had to be prayed with a book as well as beads. By the sixteenth century, the rosary had been simplified to 15 mysteries and took on the more standardized form that we know today.

Despite the fact that the format of the rosary is fairly consistent today, there are a number of variations that can be used. The greater integration of Scripture with the rosary is accomplished in several ways. Often a related passage from the Bible is read after the announcement of each mystery. The "scriptural rosary," in which a verse of the Bible is associated with each Hail Mary, is a return to the former practice of joining 150 meditative phrases to the repetitive prayers. When Pope John Paul II toward the end of his life recommended the addition of the Mysteries of Light to the rosary, he was establishing the rosary as an even fuller "compendium of the gospel."

Reflection and discussion

• Why do so many ancient traditions use prayer beads as a tool for meditation practices? In what way has the rosary enhanced my meditation?

• In what way can the rosary enhance my understanding and appreciation of the Scriptures?

The Rosary as Meditative Prayer

The rosary is essentially a contemplative prayer. Our primary focus when praying it is meditation on the joyful, luminous, sorrowful, and glorious mysteries. Rarely do the repeated prayers become our focus; they fade to the background of our consciousness as they are repeated, mantra-like, over and over again.

Meditating on the mysteries means entering the mysteries with our mind and heart—picturing the scene in our imaginations, getting inside the characters, feeling the moment with our emotions, resting in gratitude for the saving gift of the mystery. The prayer is physical and sensate as our hands finger each bead; it is verbal as we pray each prayer; it is contemplative as we enter deeply into the mystery. It seeks to bind together body and soul, mind and heart.

The rosary must never be a superficial, mechanical exercise. We need to heed the warning that Jesus offered in his Sermon on the Mount: "When you are praying, do not heap up empty phrases as the Gentiles do; for they think that they will be heard because of their many words" (Matt 6:7). Jesus is criticizing the pagan practices of reciting endless formulas in a vain attempt to force the gods to answer their petitions by saying the right verbal formulas. Repetitive prayer can become like pagan practice if it becomes an end in itself, a task to be accomplished rather than a means to deeper union with God.

The practice of contemplative prayer in every spiritual tradition teaches that there is a value in repetition. When we repeat certain phrases and even actions, like fingering prayer beads, we create a quiet rhythm within our spirits. The beating of our heart is a repetition as is the rhythm of our breathing. All of life has its rhythms, and the repetition of familiar prayers can bring our interior spirits into harmony with the divine heartbeat and the breathing of the divine Christ.

The undulation of repeated prayer can be calming and introspective. It can soothe like a lullaby and leave the mind and heart free to ascend to God, to express interior feelings and sentiments that are almost impossible to put into words. Like the repetition of "I love you" in the context of heartfelt affection, prayerful words have the power to calm and heal. Based in an intimate and personal relationship with Jesus Christ, repetitious prayer can be an important part of the language of love. The rosary can accompany us in times of joy and deep difficulty. It can be a healing prayer in times of darkness and anxiety, a lifeline in desperate moments, a place of refuge amid interior storms. It offers an opportunity to step back for a moment from the challenges of life, an easy way to come into contact with the presence of God.

We live in an age in which large numbers of people have lost any sense of the divine mysteries. The skepticism and rationalism of our modern world have eliminated from many human hearts any deep experiences of awe and wonder at the unfathomable wonders of God.

If we find our minds saturated by the images of the advertising media and society's commercialism, let us substitute some of those images with the twenty mysteries of the rosary. This type of contemplative prayer can replace that powerful imagery of modern life with the timeless mysteries of salvation. It can substitute surging feelings of competition, jealousy, and greed, with the gospel virtues of generosity, compassion, humility, and forgiveness. To meditate on the mysteries of the rosary is to grow in appreciation of divine revelation, to be transformed by the transcendent mysteries of God.

Reflection and discussion

• How can I make praying the rosary a means to deeper union with God?

• When has repetitious prayer been comforting, calming, or healing for me?

Taking Up the Rosary Anew

For many, the rosary seems to belong to the gentle piety of an age that has passed. It seems out of place in a church that is biblically grounded, liturgically manifested, and socially conscious. But when we take up the rosary anew, we realize that this ancient practice has much to teach us, and that praying this devotion can lead us to a richer understanding of the Bible, a more active participation in the liturgy, and a more committed involvement in the world.

Because the rosary is so deeply rooted in God's revelation through the Scriptures, it should invariably lead us to a richer reading and study of the Bible. Meditating on the mysteries of the rosary and reading the Bible as the word of God can both lead us to deeper union with God. Likewise, the rosary should lead us to participate more fruitfully in the liturgy. Though the rosary has less value than the public liturgy of the church, it is an ideal preparation for the liturgy of the word and Eucharist. The rosary's practice of biblical contemplation can teach us how to experience a more interior participation in the public prayers of the liturgy.

As the first and most perfect disciple—the one who heard the word of God and acted upon it like no other person in history—Mary demonstrates both the contemplative and the active dimensions of the Christian life. She listened and pondered God's word and gave it birth in the world throughout her life. In singing her Magnificat, she was a prophet announcing the coming justice of God. She is the mother of all disciples and icon of the church. With her we can stretch our hearts to take in the whole world, especially victims of injustice and violence. By praying with her while meditating on the mysteries of the rosary, we can become active contemplatives and live out more passionately our Christian vocation in the world.

The symbolism of the rosary wonderfully expresses its rich meaning. All the beads of the rosary converge on the crucifix, which represents the source and the goal of our prayers. Our devotion is always offered through Christ and, together with his eternal offering on the cross, is directed to the praise of the Father. The linking of the many beads reminds us that all people are joined together in Christ, as sons and daughters of God. Even when we pray in private, we are joined with all those we love, with those in need for whom we pray, with the family of God throughout the world, and even with the saints and angels of heaven. We are all intertwined in the common bond of Christ. The decades of beads represent the mysteries of our faith by which we are joined to God and one another. As John Henry Newman said, the rosary is a way of "holding in our hands all that we believe."

Reflection and discussion

• How can praying the rosary lead me to a richer reading and study of the Bible?

• In what way does the rosary lead me to a more active engagement with the world?

Prayer

Lord Jesus Christ, born of the Virgin Mary, you are the way, the truth, and the life. Through quiet meditation on the mysteries of the rosary, lead me in my pilgrimage of faith to an ever-deepening holiness. Help me to make space in my life for silence and contemplation, so that I can balance the images of the world with the imagery of salvation. Bring the rhythm of my life into harmony with yours, so that I can experience an ever deeper union with you, my life's destiny and greatest longing. May Mary, my mother and mother of your church, teach me and guide me to unite my life with yours.

SUGGESTIONS FOR FACILITATORS, GROUP SESSION 1

1. If the group is meeting for the first time, or if there are newcomers joining the group, it is helpful to provide nametags.

2. Ask the participants to introduce themselves and tell the group a bit about themselves. You may want to ask one or more of these introductory questions:
   • What drew you to join this group?
   • What is your biggest fear in beginning this Bible study?
   • What do you most hope to gain in this study?

3. Distribute the books to the members of the group.

4. You may want to pray this prayer as a group:

Come upon us, Holy Spirit, to enlighten and guide us as we begin this study of the mysteries of the rosary. You inspired the writers of the Scriptures to reveal the many dimensions of the mystery of Christ. Teach us, like Mary, to treasure these words and ponder them in our hearts. Motivate us to read the Scriptures, give us a love for God's word, and enflame our hearts so that we may reflect on that word and understand its truths. Bless us during this session and throughout the coming week with the fire of your love.

6. Read the Introduction aloud, pausing at each question for discussion. Group members may wish to write down the insights of the group as each question is discussed. Encourage several members of the group to respond to each question.

7. Don't feel compelled to finish the complete Introduction during the session. It is better to allow sufficient time to talk about the questions raised than to rush to the end. Group members may read any remaining sections on their own after the group meeting.

8. Instruct group members to read the first six lessons on their own during the six days before the next group meeting. They should write out their own answers to the questions as preparation for next week's group discussion.

9. Fill in the date for each group meeting under "Schedule for Group Study."

10. Conclude by praying aloud together the prayer at the end of the Introduction.

The message about the cross is foolishness to those who are perishing, but to us who are being saved it is the power of God. 1 Cor 1:18

The Sign of the Cross

1 CORINTHIANS 1:18–25; 2:1–5

¹⁸For the message about the cross is foolishness to those who are perishing, but to us who are being saved it is the power of God. ¹⁹For it is written,

"I will destroy the wisdom of the wise,
and the discernment of the discerning I will thwart."

²⁰Where is the one who is wise? Where is the scribe? Where is the debater of this age? Has not God made foolish the wisdom of the world? ²¹For since, in the wisdom of God, the world did not know God through wisdom, God decided, through the foolishness of our proclamation, to save those who believe. ²²For Jews demand signs and Greeks desire wisdom, ²³but we proclaim Christ crucified, a stumbling block to Jews and foolishness to Gentiles, ²⁴but to those who are the called, both Jews and Greeks, Christ the power of God and the wisdom of God. ²⁵For God's foolishness is wiser than human wisdom, and God's weakness is stronger than human strength.

2 ¹When I came to you, brothers and sisters, I did not come proclaiming the mystery of God to you in lofty words or wisdom. ²For I decided to know nothing among you except Jesus Christ, and him crucified. ³And I came to you in weakness and in fear and in much trembling. ⁴My speech and my proclamation were not with plausible words of wisdom, but with a demonstration of the Spirit and of power, ⁵so that your faith might rest not on human wisdom but on the power of God.

W e begin the rosary meditation by making the sign of the cross over our body, usually with the crucifix of the rosary. This profound gesture, from head to heart, and shoulder to shoulder, proclaims our redemption by the cross of Jesus Christ and our acknowledgment that by his saving cross we become partakers in the divine nature. With the sign of the cross we renew the covenant that began when we were baptized "in the name of the Father, and of the Son, and of the Holy Spirit." The grace and power of our baptism in Christ is refreshed in us. The sign of the cross summarizes the Christian faith in a single gesture: Trinity, Incarnation, and Redemption.

In the logic of human wisdom, the cross seems to express weakness, failure, and defeat (verse 18–21). In the first-century world in which Christianity began, a society in which the cross was seen as the most horrid and barbaric punishment imaginable, the gospel about a crucified Savior seemed to be utter madness. The Jews believed that God would bring salvation to the world through works of power, through a Messiah who would perform great works of liberation. The Gentile Greeks sought to discover God through reason and logic, and they followed those who used silver-tongued speech and persuasive rhetoric. For this reason, Paul says, "Jews demand signs and Greeks desire wisdom" (verse 22). But Paul and the disciples of Jesus had only one image at the heart of their message: "We proclaim Christ crucified, a stumbling block to Jews and foolishness to Gentiles" (verse 23). What seemed total foolishness to the culture of the times, Paul proclaimed as "the power of God and the wisdom of God" (verse 24). By giving himself completely for us on the cross, Jesus produced the most dramatic reversal the world has ever seen. He turned a brutal instrument of torture into the object of his followers' proudest boast: "May I never boast of anything," said Paul, "except the cross of our Lord Jesus Christ" (Gal 6:14).

In the second century, Christians commonly traced a small sign of the cross on their foreheads with their thumb or forefinger, as a sign that they learned from their baptism. The early theologian Tertullian (A.D. 160-225) wrote at the turn of the third century, "In all our travels and movements, in all our coming in and going out, in putting on our shoes, at the bath, at the table, in lighting our candles, in lying down, in sitting down, whatever employment occupies us, we mark our foreheads with the sign of the cross." John Chrysostom (347–407) wrote, "Never leave your house without making the sign of the cross." Cyril of Jerusalem (315–386) wrote, "Let us not be ashamed to confess the Crucified. Be the cross our seal made with boldness by our fingers on our brow and on everything; over the bread we eat and the cups we drink, in our comings in and goings out; when we lie down and when we awake, when we are on the road and when we are still." In the fourth century, the custom developed of signing the forehead, the lips, and the heart. The larger sign of the cross made over the body, as we practice today, developed in the East during the fifth century.

Making the sign of the cross on our bodies affirms our decision to follow Christ and states most explicitly who we are. It is a reaffirmation of our baptismal commitment to follow the teachings of Jesus and to be obedient to his commandment of loving others as he has loved us. The sign of the cross also unites us with the sufferings of Christ, making the hardships and trials of our lives an offering to the Father in union with the cross of his Son. Most of all, it proclaims for all to see that the cross is, as it was for Paul, our proudest boast.

Reflection and discussion

• Why did the symbol of the cross seem to be such embarrassing foolishness for people of the first century? What was so astounding about the boasting of Paul?

• What message am I proclaiming when I wear a cross on my neck or display a crucifix in my home?

• When do I make the sign of the cross? How can I make that gesture more meaningful for me?

• In what way is the sign of the cross a reminder and renewal of baptism? How is that connection made more explicit when the sign of the cross is made with baptismal water on our fingertips?

• In what way is the sign of the cross a radical and militant gesture?

Prayer

Lord God, help me to embrace the saving cross of Jesus Christ as the center of my life. Though it may seem foolish in the eyes of the world, I affirm that the cross is the world's greatest power and humanity's proudest boast. Help me to embrace the cross and follow in the way of Christ, in the name of the Father, and of the Son, and of the Holy Spirit.

I handed on to you as of first importance what I in turn had received. 1 Cor 15:3

The Creed of the Church

DEUTERONOMY 26:5–10 *⁵"A wandering Aramean was my ancestor; he went down into Egypt and lived there as an alien, few in number, and there he became a great nation, mighty and populous. ⁶When the Egyptians treated us harshly and afflicted us, by imposing hard labor on us, ⁷we cried to the Lord, the God of our ancestors; the Lord heard our voice and saw our affliction, our toil, and our oppression. ⁸The Lord brought us out of Egypt with a mighty hand and an outstretched arm, with a terrifying display of power, and with signs and wonders; ⁹and he brought us into this place and gave us this land, a land flowing with milk and honey. ¹⁰So now I bring the first of the fruit of the ground that you, O Lord, have given me."*

1 CORINTHIANS 15:3–8 *³For I handed on to you as of first importance what I in turn had received: that Christ died for our sins in accordance with the scriptures, ⁴and that he was buried, and that he was raised on the third day in accordance with the scriptures, ⁵and that he appeared to Cephas, then to the twelve. ⁶Then he appeared to more than five hundred brothers and sisters at one time, most of whom are still alive, though some have died. ⁷Then he appeared to James, then to all the apostles. ⁸Last of all, as to one untimely born, he appeared also to me.*

The Apostles' Creed is normally the first prayer of the rosary, usually recited while holding the crucifix. It is commonly called a creed because its first word in Latin is *credo*, meaning "I believe." It is a summary of the principle truths of the Christian faith. Along with the Nicene Creed, recited since the fifth century in the eucharistic liturgy, the Apostles' Creed is one of several professions of faith developed in the early centuries of the church. The preaching, teaching, defending, and defining of Christian doctrine necessitated the gradual formulation of a series of statements embodying the church's basic beliefs.

The process of developing fixed creeds had its beginnings in the summaries of historical beliefs in the Old Testament. The profession of God's saving work from the book of Deuteronomy is a brief epitome of Israel's founding history (Deut 26:5–10). These declarations of God's saving works in the Hebrew Scriptures are prescribed to be recited individually or communally on religious occasions. These pronouncements almost always focus on the events of the exodus—slavery, redemption, freedom, and covenant—the foundation of Israel's faith.

The Christian creeds have their roots in the apostolic age in which the New Testament was written. In liturgy, teaching, singing, praying, and witnessing, the church increasingly gave expression to Christian faith in fixed formulas. The earliest are simple confessions, like "Jesus is Lord" (Rom 10:9). Paul describes the process of handing on the truths "of first importance" that he received from the apostles. The core of early Christian preaching centered on the death, burial, resurrection, and appearances of Christ (1 Cor 15:3–5).

Fuller articulations of the faith developed in association with Christian baptism. Some texts of Acts include the Ethiopian's statement of faith as he was baptized by Philip: "I believe that Jesus Christ is the Son of God" (Acts 8:37). Baptismal creeds developed in the second century and focused on three questions centered on belief in God the Father, Son, and Holy Spirit. Similar baptismal creeds are used today as catechumens are asked to profess their faith before baptism. The Apostles' Creed developed in Rome during the third century, when the interrogatory creed was turned into a declaratory creed. This became part of the preparation of catechumens, as the bishop handed on the creed to those preparing for baptism and they rendered it back as their own witness of faith.

The Apostles' Creed, as an articulated summary of faith, is an ancient catechism. Expressing belief in the Trinity, the life, death, and resurrection of Christ, the life of his church, and everlasting life, the creed is a sign and expression of unity among believers. To recite the creed with faith is to enter into communion with the Father, Son, and Holy Spirit, and also with the whole church throughout history and across the world.

Reflection and discussion

• Which truths of faith seemed to be the most important for Paul? Why did Paul feel so compelled to faithfully hand on these truths?

• Which needs of the early church motivated the development of the Apostles' Creed? Which articles of the creed do I most want to affirm for my belief?

Prayer

God of our ancestors, you formed your people by freeing them from slavery in Egypt and bringing them into the promised land. Through Jesus, your Son, you gave us freedom from sin and death, and you brought us into the life of your church through baptism. Help me to proclaim the truths of my baptism that unite me to your people in heaven and on earth.

Your kingdom come. Your will be done, on earth as it is in heaven. Matt 6:10

Our Father Who Art in Heaven

MATTHEW 6:5–13 *⁵"And whenever you pray, do not be like the hypocrites; for they love to stand and pray in the synagogues and at the street corners, so that they may be seen by others. Truly I tell you, they have received their reward. ⁶But whenever you pray, go into your room and shut the door and pray to your Father who is in secret; and your Father who sees in secret will reward you. ⁷"When you are praying, do not heap up empty phrases as the Gentiles do; for they think that they will be heard because of their many words. ⁸Do not be like them, for your Father knows what you need before you ask him.*

⁹"Pray then in this way:
Our Father in heaven,
hallowed be your name.
¹⁰Your kingdom come.
Your will be done,
*   on earth as it is in heaven.*
¹¹Give us this day our daily bread.
¹²And forgive us our debts,
*   as we also have forgiven our debtors.*
¹³And do not bring us to the time of trial,
*   but rescue us from the evil one."*

Alll Christian prayer is ultimately directed to the Father, through Jesus, and in union with the Holy Spirit. The Our Father is the quintessential prayer of the church, since it is the prayer that Jesus himself gave to his disciples to draw them into his own relationship with the Father. Though the prayer is also found in Luke's gospel, in a slightly different form (Luke 11:2–4), the prayer from Matthew's gospel soon dominated the church's public prayer. From the early centuries, it was taught to the catechumens along with the Apostles' Creed and it was included in the celebration of the church's Eucharist. Early documents from the beginning of the second century suggest that Christians recite the Our Father three times a day.

The prayer is divided into an address to the Father followed by seven petitions. The first three are oriented to the glory of God: that his name be sanctified, that his kingdom be established, and that his will be fulfilled. The remaining four requests present our basic needs to God: that we be nourished, forgiven of sin, protected from testing, and delivered in the struggle over evil. Saint Augustine wrote: "Run through all the words of the holy prayers in Scripture, and I do not think that you will find anything in them that is not contained and included in the Lord's Prayer."

The early Christians added a prayer of praise to the end of the Our Father given in Matthew's gospel. The additional phrase is based on the words of 1 Chronicles 29:11, "Yours, O Lord, are the greatness, the power, the glory, the victory, and the majesty; for all that is in heaven and on the earth is yours; yours is the kingdom, O Lord, and you are exalted as head above all." Though the Lord's Prayer has become the hallmark of Christian prayer through the centuries, it is thoroughly Jewish. There is nothing in it that a Jew in the time of Jesus or today would not say. It is a prayer of praise, contrition, and petition that any Jew or Christian could offer to God.

When Jesus taught his disciples to pray, he did much more than give them a simple prayer they could memorize and repeat. Jesus showed them how to address God with intimacy and trust. We can pray to God like we would speak to a loving parent, addressing God with the personal, affectionate term, Abba (Father). We should not "heap up empty phrases" when we pray. Jesus urges us to pray with confidence to God who sees into our hearts and knows all about us (verses 7–8). This prayer of Jesus is the model of all prayer because Jesus knows in his own human heart the deepest needs of humanity and reveals them to us. In giving us this prayer, he gives us not only words but his own Spirit to pray them.

Reflection and discussion

• What makes prayer sincere and genuine? Why does Jesus urge us not to "heap up empty phrases" when we pray?

• What aspects of the Our Father do I notice when I imagine the prayer coming from the heart and lips of Jesus?

• As I slowly pray each phrase of the Lord's Prayer, which phrase strikes me as one I want to linger over today?

Prayer

Father in heaven, may your name be holy. Though you know my needs even before I ask for them, you still desire me to pray to you. May the kingdom, the power, and the glory be yours, now and forever.

"Blessed are you among women, and blessed is the fruit of your womb."

Luke 1:42

Hail Mary, Full of Grace

LUKE 1:26–31; 39–45 [26] *In the sixth month the angel Gabriel was sent by God to a town in Galilee called Nazareth,* [27] *to a virgin engaged to a man whose name was Joseph, of the house of David. The virgin's name was Mary.* [28] *And he came to her and said, "Greetings, favored one! The Lord is with you."* [29] *But she was much perplexed by his words and pondered what sort of greeting this might be.* [30] *The angel said to her, "Do not be afraid, Mary, for you have found favor with God.* [31] *And now, you will conceive in your womb and bear a son, and you will name him Jesus."*

[39] *In those days Mary set out and went with haste to a Judean town in the hill country,* [40] *where she entered the house of Zechariah and greeted Elizabeth.* [41] *When Elizabeth heard Mary's greeting, the child leaped in her womb. And Elizabeth was filled with the Holy Spirit* [42] *and exclaimed with a loud cry, "Blessed are you among women, and blessed is the fruit of your womb.* [43] *And why has this happened to me, that the mother of my Lord comes to me?* [44] *For as soon as I heard the sound of your greeting, the child in my womb leaped for joy.* [45] *And blessed is she who believed that there would be a fulfillment of what was spoken to her by the Lord."*

The first half of the Hail Mary prayer is formed from verses taken from the opening chapter of Luke's gospel. It is a combination of Gabriel's greeting to Mary (verse 28) and the salutation of Elizabeth to Mary (verse 42). The words of the angel and of Elizabeth represent the joyful response of both heaven and earth to the conception of the Son of God in the womb of Mary. In reciting the Hail Mary we participate over and over again in their wonder-filled response to the mystery of Christ.

The angel's word of greeting is *chaire* in Greek, *Ave* in Latin, "Hail" in old English, and "Greetings" in contemporary English. The greeting can also be translated as "Rejoice," and is used in the Old Testament to express joy over a divine saving act: "Rejoice, O daughter of Zion" (Zech 9:9; Zeph 3:14). The word translated "favored one" is rooted in the Greek word for "favor, blessing, gift, or grace." It is a title of honor, and is rendered in Latin as *gratia plena*, or traditionally in English, "full of grace." Mary is blessed because God has chosen her for his saving plan. This divine grace or favor is confirmed by the angel: "You have found favor with God" (verse 30). Her great favor is the grace of conceiving the Son of God.

Gabriel's declaration, "The Lord is with you" (verse 28), is a pledge of God's protective and guiding presence for Mary. In the Hebrew Scriptures the words expressed God's assurances to Isaac, Jacob, Moses, Gideon, and Jeremiah in their divine callings. God assures Mary that his plans for her will be realized, no matter what obstacles she may face.

The proclamation of Elizabeth, "Blessed are you among women" (verse 42), is a form of address used in the Old Testament for women who had been instruments of God's saving will, either by bringing new hope through their children or by delivering God's people from peril. God had exalted Mary among all the women of Israel: Sarah, Rachel, Hannah, Deborah, Jael (Judg 5:24), and Judith (Jdt 13:18); for Mary had been chosen to bring to birth the hope of all the ages. Elizabeth's declaration, "and blessed is the fruit of your womb" is the blessing God promised in the Torah (Deut 28:4) to those who harkened to the voice of God.

The exalted title, "Mother of God," is a translation of the Greek designation given to Mary in the early centuries, *Theotokos*, literally, the birth-giver of God. The title is anticipated by Elizabeth's designation of Mary as "the mother of my Lord" (verse 43). She is honored because in her humanity the Lord of all humbled himself to be born into the world. In the final words of the prayer we ask Mary to pray for us that we might be drawn closer to her Son throughout our lives.

Reflection and discussion

• In what way does the Hail Mary express the joyful response of both heaven and earth to the coming of Christ in the womb of Mary?

• Why is Mary the most blessed among all the women of history? Why would I want her to pray for me?

• What part of the Hail Mary do I now understand with new insight?

Prayer

Son of God and Son of Mary, you entered our world through the humanity of the virgin mother of Nazareth. I honor your blessed mother and I exalt her among all women. May her example and her prayers guide and direct me from now until the hour of my death.

"Go therefore and make disciples of all nations, baptizing them in the name of the Father and of the Son and of the Holy Spirit." Matt 28:19

Glory Be to the Father, Son, and Holy Spirit

MATTHEW 3:13–17 *¹³Then Jesus came from Galilee to John at the Jordan, to be baptized by him. ¹⁴John would have prevented him, saying, "I need to be baptized by you, and do you come to me?" ¹⁵But Jesus answered him, "Let it be so now; for it is proper for us in this way to fulfill all righteousness." Then he consented. ¹⁶And when Jesus had been baptized, just as he came up from the water, suddenly the heavens were opened to him and he saw the Spirit of God descending like a dove and alighting on him. ¹⁷And a voice from heaven said, "This is my Son, the Beloved, with whom I am well pleased."*

MATTHEW 28:16–20 *¹⁶Now the eleven disciples went to Galilee, to the mountain to which Jesus had directed them. ¹⁷When they saw him, they worshiped him; but some doubted. ¹⁸And Jesus came and said to them, "All authority in heaven and on earth has been given to me. ¹⁹Go therefore and make disciples of all nations, baptizing them in the name of the Father and of the Son and of the Holy Spirit, ²⁰and teaching them to obey everything that I have commanded you. And remember, I am with you always, to the end of the age."*

After the Our Father, the Glory Be is the most ancient Christian prayer still in use today. The prayer is sometimes called the "doxology" (*doxa* in Greek means "glory," so doxology is a formula of praise to God, literally "glory-words"). The prayer was added to the end of the psalms in early Christian practice, and is still used today to conclude the psalms of the Liturgy of the Hours. Often the prayer is chanted and accompanied by a profound bow. The same practice is sometimes used when it is prayed at the conclusion of each decade of the rosary.

At the core of the faith of Israel is the oneness of God. The daily Jewish prayer proclaims, "Hear, O Israel, the Lord our God is one Lord" (Deut 6:4). Yet, early Christians came to understand the one God as manifested in three divine persons. This Trinitarian understanding of God is first demonstrated in Paul's writings; for example, "The grace of the Lord Jesus Christ, the love of God, and the communion of the Holy Spirit be with all of you" (2 Cor 13:13).

The baptism of Jesus demonstrates the relationship and unity of the Father, Son, and Holy Spirit. The voice from heaven reveals Jesus as "my Son, the Beloved" (3:17), expressing the Father's unbounded love for his Son. The Spirit descends from the opening in the heavens to anoint Jesus as the Messiah. The unity of the one God is not broken by the trinity of persons because they are joined in perfect knowledge and love. The Trinitarian nature of God is a great mystery that we cannot completely understand, yet God invites us to share in it through our own baptism. The baptism of Jesus foreshadows Christian baptism "in the name of the Father and of the Son and of the Holy Spirit" (28:19). In baptism we are brought into this eternal relationship of love, becoming sons and daughters of the Father, brothers and sisters of Jesus Christ, in the unity of the Holy Spirit.

Glorifying the Trinity at the end of each mystery of the rosary raises our minds to the heights of heaven. United with God so profoundly through baptism, we can indeed give glory to the Father, and to the Son, and to the Holy Spirit. Singing praise to the Trinity is the natural Christian response to each of the saving events that God has accomplished in his Son. We praise God for coming among us in his Son through the power of the Holy Spirit in the life of Mary. We give praise for the ways that Christ has manifested the truth and love of the Father throughout his life because of the work of the Spirit within him. We glorify our God for pouring out the Holy Spirit into our world through the saving death and resurrection of his Son for us. Through that Spirit we too become God's Beloved, experiencing within ourselves the depths of God's love and favor for his Son.

Reflection and discussion

• Why is the Glory Be a natural response to each of the saving mysteries of the rosary?

• How does the baptism of Jesus in the Jordan demonstrate the unity of our trinitarian God?

• In what way do I participate in the life of the Trinity through my baptism in the name of the Father, Son, and Holy Spirit?

Prayer

Lord God, Holy Trinity, you invite me to share deeply in your life and experience the intimacy of your love. Glory be to the Father, and to the Son, and to the Holy Spirit, as it was in the beginning, is now, and ever shall be, world without end.

I pray that you may have the power to comprehend, with all the saints, what is the breadth and length and height and depth, and to know the love of Christ that surpasses knowledge. Eph 3:18–19

Kneeling Before the Father

EPHESIANS 3:14–21 *¹⁴For this reason I bow my knees before the Father, ¹⁵from whom every family in heaven and on earth takes its name. ¹⁶I pray that, according to the riches of his glory, he may grant that you may be strengthened in your inner being with power through his Spirit, ¹⁷and that Christ may dwell in your hearts through faith, as you are being rooted and grounded in love. ¹⁸I pray that you may have the power to comprehend, with all the saints, what is the breadth and length and height and depth, ¹⁹and to know the love of Christ that surpasses knowledge, so that you may be filled with all the fullness of God.*

²⁰Now to him who by the power at work within us is able to accomplish abundantly far more than all we can ask or imagine, ²¹to him be glory in the church and in Christ Jesus to all generations, forever and ever. Amen.

There are lots of reasons for reading the Bible and praying the rosary. We might want to know more of the truths of God's revelation, to better understand the events of the Scriptures, to pray for ourselves and other people, or to relieve our fears and anxieties. But we miss the fullest purpose of reading Scripture and practicing methods of prayer if we are only thinking about words and saying prayer formulas. The truest function of God's revelation and of all Christian prayer is to lead us to a deeper sharing in the very life of God. Paul's prayer in his letter to the Ephesians expresses this purpose as being "filled with all the fullness of God" (verse 19).

Paul describes this sharing in God's life as a relationship with the Father, the Son, and the Holy Spirit. God the Father is the creator of every community in heaven and on earth, before whom we kneel in adoration and prayer (verse 14–15). Out of the glorious riches of God's very being, the Holy Spirit imparts power to strengthen us within (verse 16). Through our response to God in faith, Christ takes up residence in the believer's heart, dwelling in our inmost being (verse 17). Through this relationship with the Father, Son, and Spirit, God works within our lives so that we might share his own life more fully.

Paul uses a botanical and architectural metaphor when he says we are being "rooted and grounded in love" (verse 17). Love is the soil into which the roots of our lives grow; love is the foundation on which the structure of our lives is built. Those who are strengthened by the Holy Spirit and in whom Christ dwells will have their lives rooted and grounded in love. The ability to comprehend "the breadth and length and height and depth" of God's life (verse 18) depends more on love than on knowledge. Growing in God's life means deepening our union in the love of God.

Whenever we pray to the Father, through the love of Christ, in the power of the Holy Spirit, we are praying in union "with all the saints" both in heaven and on earth. The realm of God's life extends beyond the horizontal, earthly community and includes the vertical community of heaven. We are part of a sacred community with transcendent boundaries. When we deepen our loving union with God through prayer, God "is able to accomplish abundantly far more than all we can ask or imagine" (verse 20).

When we pray the rosary or prayerfully read the Scriptures, our truest goal is to enter more fully into the life of God. To comprehend the mysteries of Christ has much more to do with love than with knowledge (verse 19). The value of meditating on the mysteries of the rosary or prayerfully reading the Scriptures is that it takes us beyond the words. We place ourselves in a state in which we allow God to work within us, to bring us to an experience of deeper, divine life. We expand our comprehension of the breadth, length, height, and depth of God's life and we allow God to do within us more than we could ever imagine.

Reflection and discussion

• What are some good reasons to pray the rosary? What is the best reason?

• How does biblical meditation lead us beyond knowledge and into an experience of God's love?

• What experience have I had of God being "able to accomplish abundantly far more than all we can ask or imagine"?

Prayer

Father of heaven and earth, help me to comprehend the breadth, length, height, and depth of your plan as I meditate on the mysteries of the rosary. You are able to accomplish within me far more than I can ask or imagine. Fill my heart with the love of Christ and my inmost being with the power of your Holy Spirit.

SUGGESTIONS FOR FACILITATORS, GROUP SESSION 2

1. If there are newcomers who were not present for the first group session, introduce them now.

2. You may want to pray this prayer as a group:

Lord God, your revealed and inspired word has given us the prayers of our church: the sign of the cross, the Our Father, Hail Mary, Glory Be, and the Apostles' Creed. Help us to treasure these prayers of our tradition and to pray them with trust and dedication. We are part of a sacred community with transcendent boundaries, and whenever we pray, we join with all the saints of heaven and earth. Keep us rooted and grounded in love as we study the sacred Scriptures so that we can know the love of Christ which surpasses all understanding and can accomplish within us far more than we can ask or imagine.

3. Ask one or more of the following questions:
   • What was your biggest challenge in Bible study over this past week?
   • What did you learn about prayer this week?

4. Discuss lessons 1 through 6 together. Assuming that group members have read the Scripture and commentary during the week, there is no need to read it aloud. As you review each lesson, you might want to briefly summarize the Scripture passage of each lesson and ask the group what stands out most clearly about the commentary.

5. Choose one or more of the questions for reflection and discussion from each lesson to talk over as a group. You may want to ask group members which question was most challenging or helpful to them as you review each lesson.

6. Keep the discussion moving, but don't rush the discussion in order to complete more questions. Allow time for the questions that provoke the most discussion.

7. Remember that there are no definitive answers for these discussion questions. The insights of group members will add to the understanding of all. None of these questions requires an expert.

8. Instruct group members to complete lessons 7 through 12 on their own during the six days before the next group meeting. They should write out their own answers to the questions as preparation for next week's session.

9. Conclude by praying aloud together the prayer at the end of lesson 6, or any other prayer you choose.

Sing aloud, O daughter Zion; shout, O Israel! Rejoice and exult with all your heart, O daughter Jerusalem! Zeph 3:14

The Joyful Mysteries

ZEPHANIAH 3:14–20 *¹⁴Sing aloud, O daughter Zion; shout, O Israel! Rejoice and exult with all your heart, O daughter Jerusalem! ¹⁵The Lord has taken away the judgments against you, he has turned away your enemies. The king of Israel, the Lord, is in your midst; you shall fear disaster no more. ¹⁶On that day it shall be said to Jerusalem: Do not fear, O Zion; do not let your hands grow weak. ¹⁷The Lord, your God, is in your midst, a warrior who gives victory; he will rejoice over you with gladness, he will renew you in his love; he will exult over you with loud singing ¹⁸as on a day of festival. I will remove disaster from you, so that you will not bear reproach for it. ¹⁹I will deal with all your oppressors at that time. And I will save the lame and gather the outcast, and I will change their shame into praise and renown in all the earth. ²⁰At that time I will bring you home, at the time when I gather you; for I will make you renowned and praised among all the peoples of the earth, when I restore your fortunes before your eyes, says the Lord.*

JOHN 1:1–14 *¹In the beginning was the Word, and the Word was with God, and the Word was God. ²He was in the beginning with God. ³All things came into being through him, and without him not one thing came into being. What has come into being ⁴in him was life, and the life was the light of all people. ⁵The light shines in the darkness, and the darkness did not overcome it. ⁶There was a man sent from God, whose name was John. ⁷He came as a witness to testify to the* *light, so that all might believe through him. ⁸He himself was not the light, but he came to testify to the light. ⁹The true light, which enlightens everyone, was coming into the world.*

¹⁰He was in the world, and the world came into being through him; yet the world did not know him. ¹¹He came to what was his own, and his own people did not accept him. ¹²But to all who received him, who believed in his name, he gave power to become children of God, ¹³who were born, not of blood or of the will of the flesh or of the will of man, but of God.

¹⁴And the Word became flesh and lived among us, and we have seen his glory, the glory as of a father's only son, full of grace and truth.

The five joyful mysteries of the rosary express the joy radiating from the coming of Christ into the world. Gabriel's greeting to Mary, in the first mystery, invites her to experience the joy of the Messiah's coming, "Rejoice, Mary" (Luke 1:28). The second mystery expresses the delight of Mary's visit to Elizabeth. Mary's voice and the presence of Christ in her womb caused the child in Elizabeth's womb to leap for joy (Luke 1:44). The birth of Christ in Bethlehem, the third mystery, is filled with joyfulness. The angel's announcement of the Savior's birth is described as "good news of great joy" (Luke 2:10). The fourth mystery, the presentation of Jesus in the temple of Jerusalem, is marked by the gladness of Simeon and Anna. They understood that the long awaited visitation of God to his people was being accomplished in the coming of Jesus (Luke 2:28–32). The finding of Jesus in the temple in his late childhood, the fifth mystery, further expresses the joyful awareness that this teacher of divine wisdom would devote his life totally to God (Luke 2:49).

Through the prophet Zephaniah, God had urged his people to patiently await the day that he will come to save them: "Wait for me, says the Lord" (Zeph 3:8). God promised not to forget "the remnant of Israel," "a people humble and lowly" (Zeph 3:12–13). Urging them to trust, God anticipates that day with the joyful song that closes Zephaniah's prophecy. The song is addressed to "daughter Zion" and urges her to "rejoice and exult with all your heart" (Zeph 3:14). God too will express great joy when he comes to redeem his people: "He will rejoice over you with gladness" (Zeph 3:17).

The gospel of Luke presents the people of its opening chapters as the remnant of Israel: Zechariah, Elizabeth, Mary, Joseph, the shepherds, Simeon, and Anna. These are the humble and lowly ones who wait with longing for the coming of God's salvation. The angel's salutation to Mary is the long awaited announcement to all the remnant of faithful ones, in Israel and later in the church, who wait for the word of God to come true in the world. The whole history of salvation had been leading up to the greeting of Gabriel to Mary. This daughter of Zion represents the humble and lowly ones who wait for the coming of the Lord in their midst. The angelic invitation to rejoice is the acknowledgement that the expected time has come.

Meditating on the joyful mysteries means focusing on the source and meaning of Christian joy. They all introduce us to the wonderful truth that "the Word became flesh and lived among us" (John 1:14). In the Incarnation the Son of God entered fully into our world, our history, our lives. Mary helps us discover this true joy in our heart, showing us that our faith is first and foremost the "good news" that God has come to save us. We rejoice with her that God has looked with favor on his humble and lowly ones.

Reflection and discussion

• Why are the first five mysteries called "joyful"? In what way can meditating on these mysteries increase my joy?

• What is most hopeful about Zephaniah's song of joy? How does Luke's gospel demonstrate the fulfillment of the prophet's words?

Prayer

Lord God of Israel, you taught your people to wait with patient hope for the coming of their Savior, Jesus Christ. As I reflect on the joyful myster-ies of salvation, give me a joyful confidence that you are truly with us through the presence of your divine Son.

"Do not be afraid, Mary, for you have found favor with God. And now, you will conceive in your womb and bear a son, and you will name him Jesus." Luke 1:30

The Annunciation of the Angel to Mary

LUKE 1:26–38 *²⁶In the sixth month the angel Gabriel was sent by God to a town in Galilee called Nazareth, ²⁷to a virgin engaged to a man whose name was Joseph, of the house of David. The virgin's name was Mary. ²⁸And he came to her and said, "Greetings, favored one! The Lord is with you." ²⁹But she was much perplexed by his words and pondered what sort of greeting this might be. ³⁰The angel said to her, "Do not be afraid, Mary, for you have found favor with God. ³¹And now, you will conceive in your womb and bear a son, and you will name him Jesus. ³²He will be great, and will be called the Son of the Most High, and the Lord God will give to him the throne of his ancestor David. ³³He will reign over the house of Jacob forever, and of his kingdom there will be no end." ³⁴Mary said to the angel, "How can this be, since I am a virgin?" ³⁵The angel said to her, "The Holy Spirit will come upon you, and the power of the Most High will overshadow you; therefore the child to be born will be holy; he will be called Son of God. ³⁶And now, your relative Elizabeth in her old age has also conceived a son; and this is the sixth month for her who was said to be barren. ³⁷For nothing will be impossible with God." ³⁸Then Mary said, "Here am I, the servant of the Lord; let it be with me according to your word." Then the angel departed from her.*

The first joyful mystery of the rosary is the culmination of a long history of waiting and yearning by the people of the covenant for the time of the Messiah's coming. The announcement of the angel that Mary was chosen to be the mother of Israel's Messiah signaled that the long-awaited time was at hand. The young woman from the village of Nazareth would carry in her womb all of Israel's deepest hopes. Mary would be the threshold through which the Lord would enter our world in the flesh.

God's intervention in the life of Mary was unlike anything ever before in salvation history. In the Hebrew Scriptures the announcement of a special birth was usually made to an elderly couple, often after a lifetime of longing for a child. The revelation that Mary was a young virgin highlights the utter newness of this divine action (verse 27). God was doing an extraordinarily new thing in response to the watchful yearning of his people. Mary's conception by the Holy Spirit (verse 35) was a unique and astonishing creative action, as new as God's original creation.

The heart of the annunciation scene declares the identity of the child to be born. His origin is from Israel as King David's heir and from God as the divine Son. He would be the Messiah, the one who would be given the throne of David with an unending kingdom (verses 32–33), and he would be the Son of God, because he would be conceived through the overshadowing power of God's Holy Spirit (verse 35). His name would be Jesus (verse 31), a name that means "the Lord is salvation," revealing his redemptive mission.

God was inviting Mary into a relationship with the Father, Son, and Holy Spirit, an experience that would later be universally shared by all believers. "The Most High," the "Son of God," and "the Holy Spirit," described as the Trinity in later doctrine, are present here at this climactic moment of saving grace. Mary is the first to experience this intimacy with the triune God which is the privileged calling of all Christian believers.

Many meditative reflections and visual depictions of the annunciation fail to express the turbulence, upheaval, and life-altering experience that would result from conceiving this child. We imagine the moment to be quiet, serene, and passive; but the occasion was risky, unnerving, and filled with fear. The words of the angel, "Do not be afraid" (verse 30), are reassuring to us in situations in which we, like Mary, are anxious and deeply disturbed.

Sometimes we respond begrudgingly to what we think is God's will for us. But when we recognize that the direction of our lives is planned by the One who knows us best, we realize that his plan for our lives always corresponds to our heart's deepest and most noble desires, to what will truly bring us fulfillment. In consenting to God's will, Mary did not deny herself; rather she found her truest self. As we meditate on God's action within Mary's life, we can know the personal truth of what the angel declared, "Nothing will be impossible with God" (verse 37). As we respond to God's will, we open our lives more widely to admit the God of all possibility.

Reflection and discussion

• How is the annunciation to Mary the beginning of a new era in the relationship of God to the world?

• In what ways does God announce his will for my life? What announcement have I received from God lately?

Prayer

Descend, O Holy Spirit of life, and create within me a willingness to do your will and to be my truest self. Through the angel, you declared that nothing is impossible with God. Fill me with divine grace and open my life to new possibilities.

Surely, from now on all generations will call me blessed; for the Mighty One has done great things for me, and holy is his name. Luke 1:48–49

The Visitation of Mary to Elizabeth

LUKE 1:39–56 *[39]In those days Mary set out and went with haste to a Judean town in the hill country, [40]where she entered the house of Zechariah and greeted Elizabeth. [41]When Elizabeth heard Mary's greeting, the child leaped in her womb. And Elizabeth was filled with the Holy Spirit [42]and exclaimed with a loud cry, "Blessed are you among women, and blessed is the fruit of your womb. [43]And why has this happened to me, that the mother of my Lord comes to me? [44]For as soon as I heard the sound of your greeting, the child in my womb leaped for joy. [45]And blessed is she who believed that there would be a fulfillment of what was spoken to her by the Lord."*

[46]And Mary said,

"My soul magnifies the Lord,
  [47]and my spirit rejoices in God my Savior,
[48]for he has looked with favor on the lowliness of his servant.
  Surely, from now on all generations will call me blessed;
[49]for the Mighty One has done great things for me,
  and holy is his name.
[50]His mercy is for those who fear him
  from generation to generation.
[51]He has shown strength with his arm;

he has scattered the proud in the thoughts of their hearts.
⁵²*He has brought down the powerful from their thrones,*
and lifted up the lowly;
⁵³*he has filled the hungry with good things,*
and sent the rich away empty.
⁵⁴*He has helped his servant Israel,*
in remembrance of his mercy,
⁵⁵*according to the promise he made to our ancestors,*
to Abraham and to his descendants forever."
⁵⁶*And Mary remained with her about three months and then returned to her home.*

The second joyful mystery focuses on two pregnant women of the covenant. Mary and Elizabeth both live in simple, peasant villages and both are deeply imbued with the Scriptures and truths of their Jewish faith. One is young and full of the excitement of the future; the other is old and wise with the experience of the past. Rejoicing in each other's pregnancy and in God's power made manifest in their lives, they must have fallen in each other's arms, embracing and dancing for joy.

Elizabeth, representing the old covenant, is elderly and will have a son who will be the last great figure of ancient Israel. Mary, representing the new covenant, is young and will have a son who will usher in the new age of salvation. They find in each other an instant alliance, and their joyful unity expresses the harmony between the traditional faith of Israel and the Savior's coming.

This meeting of two pregnant women was also the meeting of their unborn children. Like the ark of the covenant in the Old Testament which manifested the presence of the Lord, Mary was the bearer of the divine presence in her womb. King David was filled with awe before the ark of the Lord; Elizabeth was filled with the Holy Spirit and amazed that the mother of the Lord would come to her (verses 41–43). As the ark was greeted with exclamations of joy, leaping, and dancing by the people of Israel, so Elizabeth rejoiced and "the child leapt in her womb" (verse 41). Even before his birth, John the Baptist was announcing and preparing the way for the coming of Christ.

Mary, the new bearer of the presence of God in the world, blossomed like a rose and her whole being unfolded with praise and thankfulness to God. As a woman of God's word, she would have been quite familiar with the many passages of the Scriptures of Israel that echo throughout her canticle (verses 46–55). Mary is the culmination of a long line of women who sing songs of praise in the Bible: Miriam (Exod 15:20–21), Deborah (Judg 5), Hannah (1 Sam 2:1–10), and Judith (Jdt 16:1–17). Her praise for what God has personally done for her widens to include what God has done for everyone throughout the generations, and especially what God is doing for all the descendants of Abraham in bringing forth the Messiah. Mary is the representative of Israel, the embodiment of the people of God. The mercy and favor God has shown to Mary exemplifies the grace God offers to all his people.

Reflection and discussion

• In what way is Mary the new ark of the covenant?

• How is Mary the embodiment of God's people? What is the connection between what God has done for her and what God wants to accomplish in the lives of all of us?

Prayer

God my Savior, you have looked upon Mary with favor, grace, and blessings, and you promised the same for all the world. Manifest your mercy, strength, and holiness in my life and from generation to generation.

"Do not be afraid; for see—I am bringing you good news of great joy for all the people: to you is born this day in the city of David a Savior, who is the Messiah, the Lord." Luke 2:10–11

The Nativity of Jesus

LUKE 2:1–14 *¹In those days a decree went out from Emperor Augustus that all the world should be registered. ²This was the first registration and was taken while Quirinius was governor of Syria. ³All went to their own towns to be registered. ⁴Joseph also went from the town of Nazareth in Galilee to Judea, to the city of David called Bethlehem, because he was descended from the house and family of David. ⁵He went to be registered with Mary, to whom he was engaged and who was expecting a child. ⁶While they were there, the time came for her to deliver her child. ⁷And she gave birth to her firstborn son and wrapped him in bands of cloth, and laid him in a manger, because there was no place for them in the inn.*

⁸In that region there were shepherds living in the fields, keeping watch over their flock by night. ⁹Then an angel of the Lord stood before them, and the glory of the Lord shone around them, and they were terrified. ¹⁰But the angel said to them, "Do not be afraid; for see—I am bringing you good news of great joy for all the people: ¹¹to you is born this day in the city of David a Savior, who is the Messiah, the Lord. ¹²This will be a sign for you: you will find a child wrapped in bands of cloth and lying in a manger." ¹³And suddenly there was with the angel a multitude of the heavenly host, praising God and saying,

¹⁴"Glory to God in the highest heaven,
*   and on earth peace among those whom he favors!"*

The images of the third joyful mystery have become so familiar to us from Christmas cards that we overlook the incredible mystery of Christ's birth. The drama that took place in the out-of-the-way town of Bethlehem soon assumed center stage in the world's history. God paired a vibrant, adolescent girl and a faithful carpenter from Nazareth, and the tiny child born to them in the city of David was the Savior, Messiah, and Lord (verse 11).

The imagery of the Christmas mystery was not tranquil and serene. From God's perspective it was a divine descent into a harsh, turbulent, unredeemed world. To the Roman overlords who ordered the registration of their subjects, the humble family meant no more than three anonymous marks on the census. Because there was room for them nowhere else, Mary wrapped her newborn baby and laid him in a manger—a feeding trough for animals. Shortly the family would be political refugees, fleeing the homicidal rage of a ruthless ruler. The full reality of evil operating in the human race is clearly manifested in the oppression, poverty, and danger into which Christ was born.

One might have thought that the birth of King David's heir would have been announced to the religious scholars and leaders of the day. But God's angel reported this earth-shattering event straightaway to shepherds in the field, poor transients who were accustomed to being marginalized. These loners were not used to being included in human plans, much less those of heaven's Lord. That God would announce the birth of Christ to these shepherds indicates that this is indeed good news "for all the people" (verse 11). This is not selective news designed to keep the elite informed. The announcement to the shepherds indicates that God has truly "lifted up the lowly" (1:52) and offers to oppressed people everywhere the "good news of great joy." Christ came into this world in which there was no room for him at all; he came to be with the weak, the rejected, the discredited, with those for whom there is no room.

The Son of Mary is truly the Son of God. The round globe of Mary's belly, as full as the earth, gave birth to the life that filled up the whole world. His first cry shattered the darkness of that first Christmas night, and with his first breath all God's promises have come true. The little town of Bethlehem became the focus of heaven and earth. The angels gave glory to God who reigns in heaven and they evoked peace for the people of the earth (verse 14). Both his poverty and his sovereignty invite us to come to him. Because he did not come to us in regal bearing and royal power, we can come to him unembarrassed in rags and tags. Because he became like us, we can become like him.

Reflection and discussion

• In what way was the birth of Jesus less peaceful than most Christmas cards indicate?

• Why would God want the Savior's birth announced first to shepherds?

• What is most amazing to me about the nativity of Jesus?

Prayer

Lord God, in the birth of your Son you have wrapped your love in the flesh and blood of our humanity. He was presented to the world in a lowly manger and announced to humble shepherds. May every breath I take and every prayer I make give glory to the one called Savior, Messiah, and Lord.

Simeon blessed them and said to his mother Mary, "This child is destined for the falling and the rising of many in Israel, and to be a sign that will be opposed so that the inner thoughts of many will be revealed—and a sword will pierce your own soul too." Luke 2:34–35

The Presentation of Jesus in the Temple

LUKE 2:22–38 [22]*When the time came for their purification according to the law of Moses, they brought him up to Jerusalem to present him to the Lord* [23]*(as it is written in the law of the Lord, "Every firstborn male shall be designated as holy to the Lord"),* [24]*and they offered a sacrifice according to what is stated in the law of the Lord, "a pair of turtledoves or two young pigeons."*

[25]*Now there was a man in Jerusalem whose name was Simeon; this man was righteous and devout, looking forward to the consolation of Israel, and the Holy Spirit rested on him.* [26]*It had been revealed to him by the Holy Spirit that he would not see death before he had seen the Lord's Messiah.* [27]*Guided by the Spirit, Simeon came into the temple; and when the parents brought in the child Jesus, to do for him what was customary under the law,* [28]*Simeon took him in his arms and praised God, saying,*

[29]*"Master, now you are dismissing your servant in peace, according to your word;*

[30]*for my eyes have seen your salvation,*

[31]*which you have prepared in the presence of all peoples,*

[32]*a light for revelation to the Gentiles*

and for glory to your people Israel."

³³ *And the child's father and mother were amazed at what was being said about him.* ³⁴ *Then Simeon blessed them and said to his mother Mary, "This child is destined for the falling and the rising of many in Israel, and to be a sign that will be opposed* ³⁵ *so that the inner thoughts of many will be revealed—and a sword will pierce your own soul too."*

³⁶ *There was also a prophet, Anna the daughter of Phanuel, of the tribe of Asher. She was of a great age, having lived with her husband seven years after her marriage,* ³⁷ *then as a widow to the age of eighty-four. She never left the temple but worshiped there with fasting and prayer night and day.* ³⁸ *At that moment she came, and began to praise God and to speak about the child to all who were looking for the redemption of Jerusalem.*

The setting of the fourth joyful mystery is the temple in Jerusalem. Forty days after the birth of Jesus, Mary and Joseph brought Jesus to the temple to perform the rituals for mother and child prescribed in the law of Israel. The presentation in the temple refers to two separate regulations: the purification of the mother after the birth of a child (Lev 12:1–8) and the dedication of the firstborn son to God (Exod 13:2, 12–16). If the family could not afford the prescribed lamb for an offering, they could bring "a pair of turtledoves or two young pigeons" (verse 24). The firstborn son was to be dedicated to the service of God, since God had saved the firstborn of Israel when the firstborn of Egypt all died. The parents could release the child from this demand by a symbolic redeeming act, the payment of five silver shekels (Num 18:15–16). The narrative does not indicate, however, that Jesus was redeemed from the obligations of the firstborn, hinting at his lifelong consecration to God's service.

The elderly Simeon and Anna represent ancient Israel, waiting and longing for the fulfillment of God's promises. They stand at the juncture where the old covenant meets the new, and they are able to glimpse before their death the new age of salvation that God had in store for his people through Jesus. Simeon represents the many faithful Jews who had been hoping for centuries that God would console his people and liberate them from oppression. The Holy Spirit had revealed to him that he would not die until he had seen God's Messiah (verses 25–26). Anna believed in prayerful hope that God would bring redemption. She was the end of a long line of women in Israel who are described as prophets: Miriam (Exod 15:20), Deborah (Judg 4:4), Huldah (2 Kgs 22:14), and Isaiah's wife (Isa 8:3).

As Simeon holds the six-week-old infant in his arms, he praises God for keeping his word. Like a loyal sentinel, he had kept watch all his life in expectation of the Lord's coming. Now at this turning point in history, he could be dismissed as he welcomes the salvation of all peoples (verse 29–32). Simeon's proclamation of the universal significance of Christ's salvation amazed Mary and Joseph and anticipated the entire ministry of Jesus and his church (verse 33).

Yet in the midst of this narrative so filled with light, joy, and hope, the words of Simeon cast a dark shadow. Within the temple dedicated to sacrificial offerings, he grasped something of the nature of Jesus' sacrificial life which would provoke opposition and bring suffering to the life of Mary and her Son (verse 34–35). The same child who will bring light and salvation to the entire world will also cause disruption and division, demanding decisions and commitment. He will be "a sign that will be opposed," laying bare the hearts of everyone (verse 34–35). The lives of all who love him and align themselves with his truth will be radically altered.

The bright joyful mysteries are all tinged with shadows of sorrow. Each mystery leads to all the others, as joy leads to sorrow and then to glory. The way from Bethlehem leads inevitably to Jerusalem. The inevitable suffering by those who attach themselves to Jesus applies first and foremost to the life of Mary, his mother and first disciple. The words of Simeon addressed to her—"a sword will pierce your own soul too" (verse 35)—expresses the heart-rending pain she will experience as the first to hear and accept God's salvation manifested in her newborn child.

Reflection and discussion

• What did God reveal to Simeon about the child he held in his arms?

• What do Simeon and Anna teach me about the value of waiting? What promises am I waiting to be fulfilled in my life?

• In what way does the presentation of Jesus in the temple foreshadow the sorrowful mysteries to come?

• How are the joys of my life tempered with the possibility of loss? How are my sorrows made bearable by hope?

Prayer

Lord God, Simeon and Anna waited for the manifestation of your Son in the temple. Teach me how to wait with patient and joyful hope for the fulfillment of your promises. Open my eyes to see your salvation in the coming of Jesus to me.

"Why were you searching for me? Did you not know that I must be in my Father's house?" Luke 2:49

The Finding of Jesus in the Temple

LUKE 2:41–51 *⁴¹Now every year his parents went to Jerusalem for the festival of the Passover. ⁴²And when he was twelve years old, they went up as usual for the festival. ⁴³When the festival was ended and they started to return, the boy Jesus stayed behind in Jerusalem, but his parents did not know it. ⁴⁴Assuming that he was in the group of travelers, they went a day's journey. Then they started to look for him among their relatives and friends. ⁴⁵When they did not find him, they returned to Jerusalem to search for him. ⁴⁶After three days they found him in the temple, sitting among the teachers, listening to them and asking them questions. ⁴⁷And all who heard him were amazed at his understanding and his answers. ⁴⁸When his parents saw him they were astonished; and his mother said to him, "Child, why have you treated us like this? Look, your father and I have been searching for you in great anxiety." ⁴⁹He said to them, "Why were you searching for me? Did you not know that I must be in my Father's house?" ⁵⁰But they did not understand what he said to them. ⁵¹Then he went down with them and came to Nazareth, and was obedient to them. His mother treasured all these things in her heart.*

The fifth joyful mystery centers on the only event in the gospels from the boyhood of Jesus. At the age of twelve, he accompanied his parents to Jerusalem for the annual feast of the Passover. For that religious journey, pilgrims usually traveled in caravans along with relatives and neighbors from their village, both for company and for safety. In such large traveling groups it is not surprising that an adolescent would be missing for a day while he was assumed to be with his cousins and friends.

The frantic search for Jesus that followed his parent's discovery that he was missing and the anxious relief that followed their finding him in the temple was the occasion for the first of only two conversations we hear between Mary and Jesus in the gospels. Like any mother would, Mary scolds Jesus: "Child, why have you treated us like this? Look, your father and I have been searching for you in great anxiety" (verse 48). The response of Jesus, "Did you not know that I must be in my Father's house?" (verse 49), indicates a deep sense of identity and understanding of his life's purpose. Though Mary did not completely understand what Jesus said about directing his life to the Father (verse 50), she "treasured all these things in her heart" (verse 51).

At some point in the life of every child, parents realize that their child does not belong to them. Parents have the joy of seeing their children grow, along with the sorrow of knowing that childhood has fled. On a human level, Mary and Joseph realized that Jesus was beginning to experience that natural stage of asserting independence from parents called adolescence. On another level, they realized that the life of Jesus was to be focused on being with the Father and obediently doing his will. Jesus was truly Son of Mary and Son of God, so his sense of family went beyond kinship. His truest family would be those who honor God's authority above all others.

This final joyful mystery also prefigures the coming mysteries of light, sorrow, and glory. The adult life of Jesus culminates in another pilgrimage to Jerusalem for the feast of Passover. There he will enter the temple and amaze many with his understanding and his answers to their questions. Jesus was never truly lost; instead he was in the place where he most belonged. His ultimate destiny was being with the Father. In this final journey to Jerusalem, Jesus is again separated from his mother. Again she felt the pains of not fully understanding the tragic suffering of her son, yet trusting that Jesus must be about the work of his Father. And just as Mary found Jesus after three days as a child in Jerusalem, she will find him again after three days when he is raised by the Father to new life.

Reflection and discussion

• In what way does this passage demonstrate the transition of Jesus from childhood to adult ministry?

• What things did Mary treasure in her heart? How can I imitate the maternity and discipleship of Mary?

• In what way have I "lost" Jesus at one or more periods of my life? How did I "find" him again at the center of my life?

Prayer

Lord God, your Son learned that his work was your will and his home was with you. Instill the wisdom of your Spirit within me so that I will do your work and seek my home with you. Help me treasure the words and works of Jesus in my heart.

SUGGESTIONS FOR FACILITATORS, GROUP SESSION 3

1. Welcome group members and ask if there are any announcements anyone would like to make.

2. You may want to pray this prayer as a group:

God ever faithful, the joyful mysteries of the rosary express the joy of Christ's coming into the world. The annunciation to Mary, her visitation to Elizabeth, the birth of Christ, the presentation of Jesus in the temple, and the finding of Jesus in the temple express the fact that Israel's long wait was ending and God's promised salvation was coming. Zechariah, Elizabeth, Mary, Joseph, the shepherds, Simeon, and Anna, the faithful ones who wait, now experience salvation's dawning. Help me to learn from them how to wait with patient longing and with joyful hope.

3. Ask one or more of the following questions:

   • What new insight into the joyful mysteries did you gain this week?
   • What encouragement do you need to continue on the path of Bible reading?

4. Discuss lessons 7 through 12. Choose one or more of the questions for reflection and discussion from each lesson to talk over as a group. You may want to ask group members which question was most challenging or helpful to them as you review each lesson.

5. Keep the discussion moving, but don't rush it in order to complete more questions. Allow time for the questions that provoke the most discussion.

6. After talking about each lesson, instruct group members to complete lessons 13 through 18 on their own during the six days before the next group meeting. They should write out their own answers to the questions as preparation for next week's discussion.

7. Ask the group if anyone is having any particular problems with his or her Bible study during the week. You may want to share advice and encouragement within the group.

8. Conclude by praying aloud together the prayer at the end of one of the lessons discussed. You may add to the prayer based on the sharing that has occurred in the group.

The people who walked in darkness have seen a great light; those who lived in a land of deep darkness—on them light has shined. Isa 9:2

The Luminous Mysteries

ISAIAH 9:1–4 ¹*But there will be no gloom for those who were in anguish. In the former time he brought into contempt the land of Zebulun and the land of Naphtali, but in the latter time he will make glorious the way of the sea, the land beyond the Jordan, Galilee of the nations.*

²*The people who walked in darkness*
  have seen a great light;
those who lived in a land of deep darkness—
  on them light has shined.
³*You have multiplied the nation,*
  you have increased its joy;
they rejoice before you
  as with joy at the harvest,
  as people exult when dividing plunder.
⁴*For the yoke of their burden,*
  and the bar across their shoulders,
  the rod of their oppressor,
  you have broken as on the day of Midian.

JOHN 3:16–21 ¹⁶*"For God so loved the world that he gave his only Son, so that everyone who believes in him may not perish but may have eternal life.* ¹⁷*"Indeed, God did not send the Son into the world to condemn the world, but* *in order that the world might be saved through him.* ¹⁸*Those who believe in him are not condemned; but those who do not believe are condemned already, because they have not believed in the name of the only Son of God.* ¹⁹*And this is the judgment, that the light has come into the world, and people loved darkness rather than light because their deeds were evil.* ²⁰*For all who do evil hate the light and do not come to the light, so that their deeds may not be exposed.* ²¹*But those who do what is true come to the light, so that it may be clearly seen that their deeds have been done in God."*

The five luminous mysteries of the rosary are a few of the most significant moments and themes of the public life of Jesus. They each manifest Jesus as the light of the world, shining into the shadows of human existence, shattering the darkness of sin, lies, ignorance, and evil. Christ's baptism in the Jordan River, the first mystery of light, reveals Jesus as the Father's beloved Son, the one who will baptize with the Holy Spirit and fire. The second mystery takes place at the wedding feast in Cana, thanks to the intervention of Mary. In this first of Jesus' signs in the gospel of John, Jesus changes water into an abundance of good wine and thus manifests the kind of transformation his grace can achieve in our hearts. The proclamation of the kingdom, the third mystery, shows Christ's light shining into the lives of the sick, poor, sinners, and outcasts, as they hear his call to repentance and experience his forgiveness. The fourth mystery, the transfiguration, displays the divine glory of Christ to his closest disciples, while also preparing them to witness his sacrificial love on the cross. This leads to the fifth mystery of light, the institution of the Eucharist. Preparing both for the sorrow of his death and the glory of his resurrection, Jesus gave the gift of Eucharist as a memorial of his sacrifice and a means to share in his life.

God's prophet Isaiah preached at a time of great darkness for Israel, when the land was being conquered and destroyed by the Assyrians. But in the midst of such desperation, today's verses shine out with brilliant hope. The prophet proclaims that God will rescue his people from their subjugation—from the yoke, the bar, and the rod of their oppressors (Isa 9:4). This deliverance is described as a burst of new light and new joy upon the darkness and gloom of the land (Isa 9:2–3). This light and joy would be brought to the people through the coming of a new king who would bring completeness and harmony to the kingdom under his reign. Partial fulfillment of this prophecy was experienced in the lifetime of Isaiah, through successful battles and through kings who would bring religious reform. But the wondrous period about which the prophet foretold would come in the anticipated age of the Messiah, the Coming One who would be king and savior par excellence and a great light to the people of Galilee (Isa 9:1).

In the coming of God's Son, "the light has come into the world" (John 3:19). He brings light and life into the world "in order that the world might be saved through him" (John 3:17). Meditating on the luminous mysteries means focusing on Jesus as "the light of the world" (John 8:12). As the light of Christ shone into the world, he also shines into our lives, brightening the shadows of fear, ignorance, sin, and pessimism with his radiance.

Reflection and discussion

• Why are these five mysteries called "luminous"?

• What are the dark areas of my life where I need the light of Christ to shine?

Prayer

Jesus Christ, Light of the world, you came into a world of darkness and brought the luminance of your truth, hope, and joy. I ask you to shine the warm rays of your light into the dark corners of my heart and heal me from all that prevents me from experiencing the fullness of life.

"He on whom you see the Spirit descend and remain is the one who baptizes with the Holy Spirit." John 1:33

The Baptism of Christ

MARK 1:4–11 *⁴John the baptizer appeared in the wilderness, proclaiming a baptism of repentance for the forgiveness of sins. ⁵And people from the whole Judean countryside and all the people of Jerusalem were going out to him, and were baptized by him in the river Jordan, confessing their sins. ⁶Now John was clothed with camel's hair, with a leather belt around his waist, and he ate locusts and wild honey. ⁷He proclaimed, "The one who is more powerful than I is coming after me; I am not worthy to stoop down and untie the thong of his sandals. ⁸I have baptized you with water; but he will baptize you with the Holy Spirit."*

⁹In those days Jesus came from Nazareth of Galilee and was baptized by John in the Jordan. ¹⁰And just as he was coming up out of the water, he saw the heavens torn apart and the Spirit descending like a dove on him. ¹¹And a voice came from heaven, "You are my Son, the Beloved; with you I am well pleased."

JOHN 1:32–34 *³²And John testified, "I saw the Spirit descending from heaven like a dove, and it remained on him. ³³I myself did not know him, but the one who sent me to baptize with water said to me, "He on whom you see the Spirit descend and remain is the one who baptizes with the Holy Spirit." ³⁴And I myself have seen and have testified that this is the Son of God."*

Little is known about the first three decades of the life of Jesus between his early childhood and his adult ministry. We do know, however, that John the baptizer had begun a renewal movement within Judaism in order to prepare the way for God's next intervention into the lives of his people. His was a baptism of repentance, for renouncing sin and proclaiming a changed heart. John's baptism was in anticipation of the coming of the Messiah, the one who would baptize with the Holy Spirit (Mark 1:5–8). The purpose of John's presence was to draw people to the light. He came as a witness to testify to the dawning light of Christ. As John's gospel explains: "He himself was not the light, but he came to testify to the light. The true light, which enlightens everyone, was coming into the world" (John 1:8–9).

At the beginning of his public ministry, Jesus came into the desert wilderness around the Jordan River where John was baptizing. The scene which follows is an epiphany, a moment in which God's eternal reality is revealed in a way that is visible and understandable in human terms. Jesus was not a sinner who needed to repent, but he came to the river to unite himself fully with our humanity so that he could lead us to the fullness of life. Christ's baptism has always been one of the primary icons of the Eastern church because it is a focal moment of God's manifestation to the world, and now it is the rosary's first mystery of light.

This baptismal threshold into the saving ministry of Jesus is described as a new creation, using the imagery of Genesis. In the opening verses of the creation account, there was darkness over the deep and the Spirit of God hovered over the waters. Then God said, "Let there be light; and there was light" (Gen 1:1–3). In the opening scene of the gospel, the heavens parted at the coming of the Spirit of God upon the earth. The one who is "the true light" was coming into the world. The baptism of Jesus signaled another new beginning for the world. He was the one who would bring new life to the earth.

All of the mysteries of Christ's life have their echoes in our lives as well. We are all baptized into Christ at the beginning of our Christian lives. We enter the waters and we rise up to a life that is stronger than any suffering, sin, or death. The Holy Spirit comes upon us to give us new birth, a sharing in the very life of God. We are recreated and share in a new relationship with God, the same relationship that Jesus knew with his Father. With Jesus we become the beloved children of God, and our Father says to each of us, "You are my child, my beloved; with you I am well pleased."

Reflection and discussion

• Why is the baptism of Jesus such an important icon in the Eastern church, an epiphany of God to the world, and the first mystery of light?

• In what way is the baptism of Jesus described as a new creation? In what way was the coming of Jesus a new beginning for the world?

• What does the baptism of Jesus teach me about the deeper meaning of my own baptism? How is my baptism a new creation?

Prayer

Father in heaven, you loved us so much that you sent your Son to be the light for our world. You have given us the sacrament of baptism as a mystery that initiates us into your life. I thank you for the gift of your Spirit that allows me to stand with Jesus and be called your beloved child.

Jesus did this, the first of his signs, in Cana of Galilee, and revealed his glory; and his disciples believed in him. John 2:11

The Wedding Feast at Cana

JOHN 2:1–11 *¹On the third day there was a wedding in Cana of Galilee, and the mother of Jesus was there. ²Jesus and his disciples had also been invited to the wedding. ³When the wine gave out, the mother of Jesus said to him, "They have no wine." ⁴And Jesus said to her, "Woman, what concern is that to you and to me? My hour has not yet come." ⁵His mother said to the servants, "Do whatever he tells you." ⁶Now standing there were six stone water jars for the Jewish rites of purification, each holding twenty or thirty gallons. ⁷Jesus said to them, "Fill the jars with water." And they filled them up to the brim. ⁸He said to them, "Now draw some out, and take it to the chief steward." So they took it. ⁹When the steward tasted the water that had become wine, and did not know where it came from (though the servants who had drawn the water knew), the steward called the bridegroom ¹⁰and said to him, "Everyone serves the good wine first, and then the inferior wine after the guests have become drunk. But you have kept the good wine until now." ¹¹Jesus did this, the first of his signs, in Cana of Galilee, and revealed his glory; and his disciples believed in him.*

The second luminous mystery has its setting at a wedding in the small village of Cana, down the road from Nazareth. The gospel writer notes that the mother of Jesus was there and that Jesus and his disciples had also been invited (verse 1–2). The work of Jesus at the wedding celebration is described as "the first of his signs" by which he would reveal his glory (verse

11). This miracle of delicious wine is the first means in the gospel of John to demonstrate the love and power of God manifested in Jesus. The sign points beyond the event to the truth about who Jesus is and to the kind of radical change that Jesus represented. Involvement with Jesus moves people from a life as predictable, bland, and colorless as water, to life that is vibrant, luscious, and effervescent. Jesus has come to show people the life they had been missing.

Parents never stop being parents, even after their children have grown up. Here Mary exercises her maternal role in giving birth to the adult ministry of Jesus through this first act of his public life. Just as a mother instinctively knows the time for giving birth, Mary knew when the moment was ready for Jesus to be revealed and she initiated his ministry with her words. Always watchful for opportunities to gently bring others to a belief in her Son, Mary informed Jesus, "They have no wine" (verse 3).

"Do whatever he tells you" (verse 5) are the final words of the mother of Jesus recorded in John's gospel. Her words reflect the words of the Father at the transfiguration of Jesus: "This is my Son; listen to him." Genuine obedience has nothing to do with forced compliance or unthinking submission. In both Hebrew and Greek the word translated "obedience" is rooted in the verb "to listen." Mary demonstrated with her life that obedience means carefully listening to God's word, savoring it, and then responding wholeheartedly. Through her example of listening and keeping God's word, she bore God's word into the world and taught the disciples of Jesus to do the same.

When Jesus changed the water into wine at the wedding feast, "his disciples believed in him" (verse 11), thanks to the example and intervention of Mary, the first among believers. For those who listen to him and act upon his word, life becomes an anticipation of the joyous wedding feast of God's kingdom foretold by the prophets. In Jesus, this promise of God breaks into the present moment to transform ordinary life into an experience of fine, abundant wine.

Reflection and discussion

• What is the truth about Jesus that is manifested through this "first of his signs"? Why is wine an effective symbol of life in Christ?

• How does Mary's instruction, "Do whatever he tells you," challenge me today? Am I trusting enough to do whatever Jesus tells me?

• How is my ordinary life transformed because of the presence and ministry of Jesus? How does Jesus give me hope for the future?

Prayer

Father of Jesus and Mary, the transformation of water into wine represents the saving ministry of your Son. Help me to listen and act upon your word as I hear it spoken to me through Jesus. Give me a lively hope in the glorious wedding feast you have promised.

"Strife first for the kingdom of God and his righteousness, and all these things will be given to you as well." Matt 6:33

The Proclamation of the Kingdom

MARK 1:14–15 *¹⁴Now after John was arrested, Jesus came to Galilee, proclaiming the good news of God, ¹⁵and saying, "The time is fulfilled, and the kingdom of God has come near; repent, and believe in the good news."*

MARK 2:1–12 *¹When he returned to Capernaum after some days, it was reported that he was at home. ²So many gathered around that there was no longer room for them, not even in front of the door; and he was speaking the word to them. ³Then some people came, bringing to him a paralyzed man, carried by four of them. ⁴And when they could not bring him to Jesus because of the crowd, they removed the roof above him; and after having dug through it, they let down the mat on which the paralytic lay. ⁵When Jesus saw their faith, he said to the paralytic, "Son, your sins are forgiven." ⁶Now some of the scribes were sitting there, questioning in their hearts, ⁷"Why does this fellow speak in this way? It is blasphemy! Who can forgive sins but God alone?" ⁸At once Jesus perceived in his spirit that they were discussing these questions among themselves; and he said to them, "Why do you raise such questions in your hearts? ⁹Which is easier, to say to the paralytic, 'Your sins are forgiven,' or to say, 'Stand up and take your mat and walk'? ¹⁰But so that you may know that the Son of Man has authority on earth to forgive sins" —he said to the paralytic— ¹¹"I say to you, stand up,* *take your mat and go to your home." ¹²And he stood up, and immediately took the mat and went out before all of them; so that they were all amazed and glorified God, saying, "We have never seen anything like this!"*

MATTHEW 6:25–33 *²⁵"Therefore I tell you, do not worry about your life, what you will eat or what you will drink, or about your body, what you will wear. Is not life more than food, and the body more than clothing? ²⁶Look at the birds of the air; they neither sow nor reap nor gather into barns, and yet your heavenly Father feeds them. Are you not of more value than they? ²⁷And can any of you by worrying add a single hour to your span of life? ²⁸And why do you worry about clothing? Consider the lilies of the field, how they grow; they neither toil nor spin, ²⁹yet I tell you, even Solomon in all his glory was not clothed like one of these. ³⁰But if God so clothes the grass of the field, which is alive today and tomorrow is thrown into the oven, will he not much more clothe you—you of little faith? ³¹Therefore do not worry, saying, 'What will we eat?' or 'What will we drink?' or 'What will we wear?' ³²For it is the Gentiles who strive for all these things; and indeed your heavenly Father knows that you need all these things. ³³But strive first for the kingdom of God and his righteousness, and all these things will be given to you as well."*

The third mystery of light, the proclamation of the kingdom of God, encompasses practically the entirety of Jesus' adult mission. From the beginning of his public ministry through his passion, the imminent kingdom of God was the center of Jesus' message. At the beginning he proclaimed, "The time is fulfilled, and the kingdom of God has come near; repent, and believe in the good news" (Mark 1:15). At the end of his life he said, "Truly I tell you, I will never again drink of the fruit of the vine until that day when I drink it new in the kingdom of God" (Mark 14:25).

God's kingdom is the primary biblical image that expresses God's sovereignty over all of creation and all of history. God reigns eternally, yet that reign is not yet fully expressed "on earth as it is in heaven." Jesus announced the coming of God's kingdom through his teachings and he demonstrated the imminence of God's reign by his miracles. In his parables, Jesus expressed the coming of the kingdom by teaching that the kingdom of God is like a treasure beyond price, seeds growing in a field, and a magnificent banquet. Through healing the blind, deaf, lame, and paralyzed, and by casting out demons and forgiving sins, Jesus demonstrated that the kingdom was breaking into the world (Mark 2:9–11). The kingdom, Jesus showed, is mysteriously present in Jesus himself, as he manifests the transforming power of God in the world.

The kingdom of God is brought into the world through Jesus, but it must be accepted and claimed by humanity. The first way in which we experience the coming reign of God is through repentance. When Jesus calls his listeners to "repent," he is challenging us to reorient our lives, to turn away from sin and turn back to God (Mark 1:15). The call to "believe in the good news" is the challenge to place God's saving truth at the center of our lives. Realigning our lives according to the priorities of God's kingdom, means to "strive first for the kingdom of God" (Matt 6:33). Our heavenly Father knows all of our needs, better than we know them ourselves. Food, clothing, work, and income are all important, but they cannot sustain us at the core of our being. When they become the center of our concern, we are left feeling anxious, depleted, and frustrated. When we give the sovereignty of God the first place, over all other worries and concerns, then all our needs and yearnings find a certain harmony and we can live with trusting confidence.

Reflection and discussion

• In what way is the kingdom of God both a present and a future reality?

• In what ways did Jesus demonstrate the coming of God's kingdom?

• Why was the call to repentance the first proclamation of Jesus? How is Jesus challenging me to repent and believe in the good news?

• When have I not given the reign of God first place in my life? What happens when I make anything else the central focus of life?

• How can I make the command of Jesus in Matthew 6:33 a living reality?

Prayer

Lord God, the first priority of your Son was establishing your kingdom in the world. Open my heart to repentance, help me believe the good news of your reign, and let me experience the forgiveness and healing you offer. May I always seek first the kingdom and know that the other priorities of my life will then fall in line.

Then a cloud overshadowed them, and from the cloud there came a voice,
"This is my Son, the Beloved; listen to him!" Mark 9:7

The Transfiguration
of Jesus

MARK 9:2–10 *²Jesus took with him Peter and James and John, and led them up a high mountain apart, by themselves. And he was transfigured before them, ³and his clothes became dazzling white, such as no one on earth could bleach them. ⁴And there appeared to them Elijah with Moses, who were talking with Jesus. ⁵Then Peter said to Jesus, "Rabbi, it is good for us to be here; let us make three dwellings, one for you, one for Moses, and one for Elijah." ⁶He did not know what to say, for they were terrified. ⁷Then a cloud overshadowed them, and from the cloud there came a voice, "This is my Son, the Beloved; listen to him!" ⁸Suddenly when they looked around, they saw no one with them any more, but only Jesus.*

⁹As they were coming down the mountain, he ordered them to tell no one about what they had seen, until after the Son of Man had risen from the dead. ¹⁰So they kept the matter to themselves, questioning what this rising from the dead could mean.

The fourth mystery of light, the transfiguration of Jesus on the mountain, is an anticipation of the glory of Christ that awaited his disciples on the other side of the cross. Immediately after revealing the necessity of his suffering and death, and telling his disciples of the necessity of taking up the cross in their own lives, Jesus brought his three closest disciples up a high mountain to prepare them for the difficult road ahead. Jesus offered them a glimpse of his glory to give them courage before bringing them back down the mountain to travel with him on the way to Jerusalem.

The dazzling white, the high mountain, the cloud, and the voice from the cloud were all images from the Old Testament that showed the glorious presence of God with his people. The two central figures of the Old Testament were also there: Moses, as the great lawgiver, and Elijah, representing all the prophets of old. Jesus was indeed the fulfillment of God's entire saving plan for his people, the one to whom both the law and the prophets pointed.

Peter, James, and John experienced the transfiguration of Jesus as a pure grace from God. Peter expressed the amazement and gratitude of the disciples, and he wants to prolong the grace of the moment as long as possible (verse 5). The glimpse of glory was not only a preview of what was to come; it was an insight into what has always been true. The illuminated Christ expressed his glorious divine nature, the glorious reality that Jesus is the beloved Son of God (verse 7). His radiant face and glowing garments display the glory of God that dwells in him all the time. The three privileged disciples received this visionary gift of insight which enabled them to understand and appreciate for the moment who Jesus truly is.

The voice of God from the cloud told the disciples to "listen to him" (verse 7). Genuine obedience to the word of God is only possible through listening to and savoring the words of Jesus. Listening to our own fears, to our desires for power, to the false messages of our world, to those opposed to the way of love, is failure to listen closely to Jesus. Peter, James, and John will soon demonstrate that they don't want the way of the cross. These three will fall asleep at Gethsemane, desire their own prestige, deny their relationship with Jesus, and flee from Jesus in the moment of crisis. The way of discipleship means listening to Jesus, imitating him, following him, and taking up the cross.

As they were coming down the mountain, the disciples were contemplating the experience and asking what rising from the dead could mean (verses 9–10). As we ponder and reflect on the mystery of the transfiguration, we will be able to see the glory of God present among us. In the many manifestations of Christ in our world, particularly his sacramental presence and his presence in individual people, we will be able to glimpse divine, glorious light. God washes out our eyes again and again, with tears of sorrow and tears of joy, so that we can see more clearly. With deeper vision we can perceive more clearly the truth that is always before us.

Reflection and discussion

• In what mountaintop experiences of my life have I received the grace to see God's glory most clearly?

• Why did Peter want to make three dwellings? Why do moments of transfiguration never last very long? Is there a way to prolong them?

• Am I able to see the glory of God's presence shining in the lives of other people? What would give me clearer vision?

Prayer

Glorious God, you offer to me graced moments of transfiguration when I am able to see your divine glory shining out in the people and events of my life. Cleanse my eyes and give me the insight to see and understand the truth of Jesus Christ present in our humanity.

When the hour came, he took his place at the table, and the apostles with him. He said to them, "I have eagerly desired to eat this Passover with you before I suffer; for I tell you, I will not eat it until it is fulfilled in the kingdom of God." Luke 22:14–16

The Institution of the Eucharist

LUKE 22:1–23 ¹*Now the festival of Unleavened Bread, which is called the Passover, was near.* ²*The chief priests and the scribes were looking for a way to put Jesus to death, for they were afraid of the people.*

³*Then Satan entered into Judas called Iscariot, who was one of the twelve;* ⁴*he went away and conferred with the chief priests and officers of the temple police about how he might betray him to them.* ⁵*They were greatly pleased and agreed to give him money.* ⁶*So he consented and began to look for an opportunity to betray him to them when no crowd was present.*

⁷*Then came the day of Unleavened Bread, on which the Passover lamb had to be sacrificed.* ⁸*So Jesus sent Peter and John, saying, "Go and prepare the Passover meal for us that we may eat it."* ⁹*They asked him, "Where do you want us to make preparations for it?"* ¹⁰*"Listen," he said to them, "when you have entered the city, a man carrying a jar of water will meet you; follow him into the house he enters* ¹¹*and say to the owner of the house, 'The teacher asks you, "Where is the guest room, where I may eat the Passover with my disciples?"'* ¹²*He will show you a large room upstairs, already furnished. Make preparations for us there."* ¹³*So they went and found everything as he had told them; and they prepared the*

Passover meal. [14]*When the hour came, he took his place at the table, and the apostles with him.* [15]*He said to them, "I have eagerly desired to eat this Passover with you before I suffer;* [16]*for I tell you, I will not eat it until it is fulfilled in the kingdom of God."* [17]*Then he took a cup, and after giving thanks he said, "Take this and divide it among yourselves;* [18]*for I tell you that from now on I will not drink of the fruit of the vine until the kingdom of God comes."* [19]*Then he took a loaf of bread, and when he had given thanks, he broke it and gave it to them, saying, "This is my body, which is given for you. Do this in remembrance of me."* [20]*And he did the same with the cup after supper, saying, "This cup that is poured out for you is the new covenant in my blood.* [21]*But see, the one who betrays me is with me, and his hand is on the table.* [22]*For the Son of Man is going as it has been determined, but woe to that one by whom he is betrayed!"* [23]*Then they began to ask one another, which one of them it could be who would do this.*

The final luminous mystery, the institution of the Eucharist, forms a bridge connecting the joyful and luminous mysteries with the sorrowful and glorious mysteries. The Last Supper is the final action of Christ's ministry before he enters into his passion and death. It expresses and summarizes his entire life of self-giving. Over the bread and wine of the Passover meal, Jesus says, "This is my body which is given for you" and "This cup that is poured out for you is the new covenant in my blood" (verses 19–20). As the disciples down through the ages celebrate Eucharist in his memory, they make present again in space and time the eternal offering of Christ on the cross and experience his risen presence with them. The Eucharist is the extension of the Incarnation; the Word made flesh has become flesh and blood for us, the living presence of Christ with his church. When celebrating the Eucharist, the church proclaims that Christ has died, that he is risen, and that he will come again. The last meal of Jesus, filled with betrayal, anguish, and dread about what lay ahead, is also a feast of great joy, longing, and hope for what God has promised.

In celebrating the Passover, the people of Israel always looked back in remembrance to the foundational moment of their history, when God freed them from the bondage of their servitude and brought them out to experience life as a freed people. As a memorial ritual, the Passover feast made that saving moment mystically present so that each new generation could participate in its founding event. But the Passover not only made the past present;

it also anticipated the future. It looked forward to that final salvation in which the Messiah would come to Jerusalem to liberate his people. Jesus instituted the Eucharist on the eve of Passover, offering himself as the Passover sacrifice and giving his church a means to make present his saving death and resurrection so that all could share in its grace. Like the ancient Passover, the Eucharist makes present again the foundational event of the past and anticipates its fulfillment in the kingdom of God (verses 15–18).

When Jesus instituted the Eucharist, he bound his followers into the community of the new covenant (verse 20). Whenever they offered the Eucharist in the future, they would offer their own lives to the Father in union with Christ. The prayers, works, joys, and suffering of God's people become an acceptable sacrifice to God when offered in union with the sacrifice of Christ on the cross. When we receive from the altar the body and blood of Christ, we become the mystical body of Christ for the world. We become what we eat and drink, and then go out to the world to be food for those who hunger and thirst for God.

Reflection and discussion

• In what way is Christ's gift of the Eucharist an expression and summary of his entire life of self-giving?

• What insights into the meaning of Eucharist are provided by an understanding of Israel's Passover feast?

• What is the past event made present in the Eucharist? What future event does the Eucharist anticipate?

• What do I think about when I say "Amen" while receiving the body and blood of Christ in communion?

• In what way does this fifth mystery connect the luminous mysteries with the sorrowful and glorious mysteries?

Prayer

God of the covenant, at the Last Supper Christ gave his church the Eucharist as the everlasting sacrament of his body and blood. Free me from the bondage of sin and death and join me in intimate covenant with Christ and his church. May I become what I eat and drink, and go out to bring your presence to a hungry world.

SUGGESTIONS FOR FACILITATORS, GROUP SESSION 4

1. Welcome group members and ask if anyone has any questions, announcements, or requests.

2. You may want to pray this prayer as a group:

Luminous God, the mysteries of light reveal your Son as the light of the world, shining into the shadows of our lives. Christ's baptism, the miracle of the wine at Cana, his proclamation of the kingdom, his transfiguration, and gift of the Eucharist shine the light of truth and goodness into the darkness of ignorance, sin, and evil. As we study your inspired word in the gospels, enlighten us and enliven us so that our lives may be open to the forgiveness, renewal, and sanctification you desire to give to us.

3. Ask one or more of the following questions:

   • What is the most difficult part of this study for you?
   • What new insight did you experience this week through the luminous mysteries?

4. Discuss lessons 13 through 18. Choose one or more of the questions for reflection and discussion from each lesson to discuss as a group. You may want to ask group members which question was most challenging or helpful to them as you review each lesson.

5. Keep the discussion moving, but allow time for the questions that provoke the most discussion. Encourage the group members to use "I" language in their responses.

6. After talking over each lesson, instruct group members to complete lessons 19 through 24 on their own during the six days before the next group meeting. They should write out their own answers to the questions as preparation for next week's session.

7. Conclude by praying aloud together the prayer at the end of one of the lessons discussed. You may choose to conclude the prayer by asking members to pray aloud any requests they may have.

He was wounded for our transgressions, crushed for our iniquities; upon him was the punishment that made us whole, and by his bruises we are healed.

Isa 53:5

The Sorrowful Mysteries

ISAIAH 53:1–9

[1] *Who has believed what we have heard?*
   And to whom has the arm of the Lord been revealed?
[2] *For he grew up before him like a young plant,*
   and like a root out of dry ground;
he had no form or majesty that we should look at him,
   nothing in his appearance that we should desire him.
[3] *He was despised and rejected by others;*
   a man of suffering and acquainted with infirmity;
and as one from whom others hide their faces
   he was despised, and we held him of no account.

[4] *Surely he has borne our infirmities*
   and carried our diseases;
yet we accounted him stricken,
   struck down by God, and afflicted.
[5] *But he was wounded for our transgressions,*
   crushed for our iniquities;
upon him was the punishment that made us whole,
   and by his bruises we are healed.

⁶*All we like sheep have gone astray;*
*   we have all turned to our own way,*
and the Lord has laid on him
*   the iniquity of us all.*

⁷*He was oppressed, and he was afflicted,*
*   yet he did not open his mouth;*
like a lamb that is led to the slaughter,
*   and like a sheep that before its shearers is silent,*
*   so he did not open his mouth.*
⁸*By a perversion of justice he was taken away.*
*   Who could have imagined his future?*
For he was cut off from the land of the living,
*   stricken for the transgression of my people.*
⁹*They made his grave with the wicked*
*   and his tomb with the rich,*
although he had done no violence,
*   and there was no deceit in his mouth.*

JOHN 13:1–5 ¹*Now before the festival of the Passover, Jesus knew that his hour had come to depart from this world and go to the Father. Having loved his own who were in the world, he loved them to the end.* ²*The devil had already put it into the heart of Judas son of Simon Iscariot to betray him. And during supper* ³*Jesus, knowing that the Father had given all things into his hands, and that he had come from God and was going to God,* ⁴*got up from the table, took off his outer robe, and tied a towel around himself.* ⁵*Then he poured water into a basin and began to wash the disciples' feet and to wipe them with the towel that was tied around him.*

The five sorrowful mysteries of the rosary invite us to contemplate the individual moments of Christ's passion. They are most meaningful for us in times of grief, suffering, and confusion. In these mysteries, Christ's self-giving love is displayed most fully. In his agony in the garden, the first mystery, Jesus is overwhelmed with sorrow, yet he accepts the suffering to come. The second mystery, the scourging of Christ with wounding whips, demonstrates the merciless brutality of Jesus' suffering. The crowning with thorns, the third mystery, adds mocking humiliation to his terrible agony. The fourth mystery, the journey of Jesus along the way of the cross, marks the way for every person who must walk the way of suffering. The death of Jesus, the final mystery of sorrow, is the climax of Christ's passion as well as the height of his saving love expressed so dramatically for our salvation.

No passage from the Old Testament speaks more eloquently of the mystery of Christ's suffering than the Suffering Servant song of the prophet Isaiah. This mysterious figure, spoken about by Isaiah over five hundred years before the coming of Jesus, is chosen by God to take upon himself the sin and suffering of others. This "man of suffering" seemed to be a failure, rejected and despised by others, stricken, smitten, and afflicted (Isa 53:3–4). Yet, God's Servant is innocent, and his suffering is for the sake of others: "He was wounded for our transgressions, crushed for our iniquities" (Isa 53:5). Though we had gone astray and turned away from God's love, God "has laid upon him the iniquity of us all" (Isa 53:6). In him our sin finds forgiveness, our brokenness is made whole, our spiritual illness is healed.

Like the silent lamb led to the slaughter, the Servant was quiet and unprotesting as he made his way to death (Isa 53:7). Subjected to an unjust trial, he was led from the court to his execution, cut off and stricken with a violent death. Innocent to the end, he was buried like a common criminal (Isa 53:8–9). Isaiah's prophecy gave early Christian writers insight into the meaning of Christ's suffering and death, and it offers us much to ponder about the reason for Christ' many sorrows. Though it is impossible to understand precisely how God exchanged the suffering of his Son for our forgiveness and healing, it helps us contemplate the depths of his love for us.

The final discourse of Jesus in John's gospel summarizes the meaning of Jesus' entire life and death as an act of love: "Having loved his own who were in the world, he loved them to the end" (John 13:1). "To the end" means both to the end of his life on earth, and loving them completely. His final acts before the passion, the washing of his disciples' feet and the gift of Eucharist, express his total gift of self for others. He gave himself in service to others, in sacrificial love "to the end," and he asked his disciples to do the same. As followers in the way of Jesus, we are to love "to the end"—to the end of our lives and as completely as we can love.

Reflection and discussion

• In what way do the sorrowful mysteries offer meaning and hope to the sufferings and sorrows of my life?

• At what stages in my life have the five sorrowful mysteries been most comforting?

• In what way am I called to imitate the loving self-giving of Jesus "to the end"?

Prayer

Suffering Lord, you have demonstrated your love to the end through your passion and death. I want to follow as your disciple along the way of your cross. Help me to love as you loved, to serve as you served, and to give myself as you gave yourself completely.

"Stay awake and pray that you may not come into the time of trial; the spirit indeed is willing, but the flesh is weak." Matt 26:41

The Agony in the Garden of Gethsemane

MATTHEW 26:36–46 *36 Then Jesus went with them to a place called Gethsemane; and he said to his disciples, "Sit here while I go over there and pray." 37 He took with him Peter and the two sons of Zebedee, and began to be grieved and agitated. 38 Then he said to them, "I am deeply grieved, even to death; remain here, and stay awake with me." 39 And going a little farther, he threw himself on the ground and prayed, "My Father, if it is possible, let this cup pass from me; yet not what I want but what you want." 40 Then he came to the disciples and found them sleeping; and he said to Peter, "So, could you not stay awake with me one hour? 41 Stay awake and pray that you may not come into the time of trial; the spirit indeed is willing, but the flesh is weak." 42 Again he went away for the second time and prayed, "My Father, if this cannot pass unless I drink it, your will be done." 43 Again he came and found them sleeping, for their eyes were heavy. 44 So leaving them again, he went away and prayed for the third time, saying the same words. 45 Then he came to the disciples and said to them, "Are you still sleeping and taking your rest? See, the hour is at hand, and the Son of Man is betrayed into the hands of sinners. 46 Get up, let us be going. See, my betrayer is at hand."*

The mystery of Christ's agony in Gethsemane contrasts sharply with the luminous mystery of his transfiguration. Yet in each of these events, Jesus took his three closest disciples aside from the others to reveal the depth of his mission. As Peter, James, and John had witnessed Jesus in glory on the mountaintop, they now see him in anguish and weakness in the olive grove before he faces his death. If we are to truly understand Jesus, we must, like those three disciples, meditate on his human agony as well as his divine glory.

Jesus is "deeply grieved, even to death" (verse 38), pushed to the extreme limits of fear and sadness. Fully human, he falls prostrate with his face to the ground and asks that his "cup of suffering" be removed (verse 39). Yet, at the same time, the will of Jesus is perfectly united to the Father's. So he immediately says, "Not what I want, but what you want." Jesus could have easily escaped from his arrest and passion that night by continuing up and over the Mount of Olives and into the Judean wilderness. But, while he felt a human aversion and horror at the prospect of a painful death, Jesus was completely willing to embrace that suffering for the sake of his love for humanity and carrying out his Father's plan of salvation.

Christ's "yes" in the garden of Gethsemane reversed the "no" of Adam in the garden of Eden. During Adam's time of testing in the garden he failed to trust the Father, preferring his own will to God's. But during the testing of Jesus, he trusted completely and was intent on faithfulness to the Father's will. Adam's disobedience led him to the forbidden tree; Jesus' obedient trust led him to the wood of the cross, the new tree of life. In the garden of Gethsemane, Jesus took upon himself the sin of humanity and agreed to carry it to the cross.

The fervent prayer of Jesus is strongly contrasted with the disciples' behavior. Three times Jesus returns from prayer to find them asleep. The posture of discipleship must be watchful alertness if they are to continue the mission of Jesus despite opposition. The willing spirit and the weak flesh will play out their battles in the lives of all disciples. The willing prayer of Jesus to the Father soothed his anguish and strengthened his resolve, but the disciples' neglectful drowsiness and failure to watch in vigilant prayer led to their fearful retreat when confronted with the arrest of Jesus. Jesus' counsel to "stay awake and pray" (verse 41) is a summons to all disciples not to grow weary and lax, but to be alert to the agony of Christ, in whatever person or situation, in whatever time and place.

Reflection and discussion

• What thoughts and feelings might Jesus have experienced in Gethsemane while his closest disciples slept?

• Why are the mountain of transfiguration and the garden of Gethsemane both necessary to contemplate for a full understanding of Jesus?

• How does the drowsy neglect of the disciples serve as a warning for me? How can I better "stay awake and pray"?

Prayer

Obedient Son of God, you arose from prayer in Gethsemane entrusting your life into the hands of your Father. Help me to be watchful and alert, so that I will be prepared for the hour of trial. Give me a confident trust so that I can pray with you and Mary, "Your will be done."

So Pilate, wishing to satisfy the crowd, released Barabbas for them; and after flogging Jesus, he handed him over to be crucified. Mark 15:15

The Scourging at the Pillar

MARK 15:1–15 *¹As soon as it was morning, the chief priests held a consultation with the elders and scribes and the whole council. They bound Jesus, led him away, and handed him over to Pilate. ²Pilate asked him, "Are you the King of the Jews?" He answered him, "You say so." ³Then the chief priests accused him of many things. ⁴Pilate asked him again, "Have you no answer? See how many charges they bring against you." ⁵But Jesus made no further reply, so that Pilate was amazed.*

⁶Now at the festival he used to release a prisoner for them, anyone for whom they asked. ⁷Now a man called Barabbas was in prison with the rebels who had committed murder during the insurrection. ⁸So the crowd came and began to ask Pilate to do for them according to his custom. ⁹Then he answered them, "Do you want me to release for you the King of the Jews?" ¹⁰For he realized that it was out of jealousy that the chief priests had handed him over. ¹¹But the chief priests stirred up the crowd to have him release Barabbas for them instead. ¹²Pilate spoke to them again, "Then what do you wish me to do with the man you call the King of the Jews?" ¹³They shouted back, "Crucify him!" ¹⁴Pilate asked them, "Why, what evil has he done?" But they shouted all the more, "Crucify him!" ¹⁵So Pilate, wishing to satisfy the crowd, released Barabbas for them; and after flogging Jesus, he handed him over to be crucified.

The second sorrowful mystery, the scourging of Jesus with whips, is a powerful expression of the manifold torments Jesus experienced during his passion. While the gospels only mention briefly that Jesus was scourged before being handed over for crucifixion (verse 15), readers knew the familiar details of scourging as well as they knew the particulars of crucifixion. Noting that Jesus was flogged at the hands of Pilate and his Roman soldiers convinced readers that Jesus endured the most brutal of tortures.

Beatings with wooden rods or leather whips were a severe punishment in the ancient world. Mosaic law stated that the number of lashes should be proportionate to the offence and that the maximum number of lashes that could be applied to a victim was forty (Deut 25:2–3). Jewish practice subtracted one stroke to guarantee that the limit would not be surpassed, and "forty lashes minus one" (2 Cor 11:24) became a characteristic of Jewish punishment. Roman floggings, however, had no such limitations and were generally far more brutal. Often the straps of leather used for Roman scourging were weighted at the ends with pieces of metal or bone which would rip the victim's flesh. Prisoners to be scourged were usually stripped and tied to a pillar. The scourging often served as a prelude to crucifixion, inflicting intense physical trauma and weakening the prisoner, resulting in a quicker death.

The custom of releasing a prisoner at Passover seems to have been a concession to the Jews by the Roman government. The choice between Jesus or Barabbas rested with the crowd, though they were prompted by the chief priests to call for Barabbas. He became a symbol of how God deals with our sins: taking them on himself through the death of Jesus so that we might go free and live. Barabbas's name literally means "son of the father." We are all sons and daughters of the Father, who have been freed and given life by the true Son, Jesus Christ.

After the crowd called for Barabbas, Pilate asked them what he should do with Jesus. They shouted, "Crucify him" (verses 13–14). For centuries, people have asked who is responsible for the crucifixion of Jesus. Is it the religious leaders who arrested him and plotted against his life, the disciple who betrayed him with a kiss, the armed soldiers who seized him in Gethsemane, the disciples who deserted him, the Roman procurator who handed Jesus over to please the crowds, the soldiers who scourged him, or those who hammered in the nails? When we consider that Jesus loved us to the end and was crucified for our salvation, we must realize that the shout of the crowd in Jerusalem, "Crucify him," is our cry as well.

Reflection and discussion

• When have I had to watch someone I love suffer? How might Barabbas have felt as he knew that Jesus suffered in his place?

• Why is it impossible to blame any one group of people for the passion and death of Jesus?

• Why is our world so saturated with violence, hostility, and rage? In what ways do I compromise my beliefs or remain silent in the face of injustices?

Prayer

Jesus, you submitted to brutal violence and took upon yourself the guilt of us all. I cringe in horror at the injustices done to you by those whose lives were controlled by anger and rage. Help me to work for justice for inno-cent victims everywhere.

The soldiers wove a crown of thorns and put it on his head, and they dressed him in a purple robe. John 19:2

The Crowning With Thorns

MATTHEW 27:27–31 *²⁷Then the soldiers of the governor took Jesus into the governor's headquarters, and they gathered the whole cohort around him. ²⁸They stripped him and put a scarlet robe on him, ²⁹and after twisting some thorns into a crown, they put it on his head. They put a reed in his right hand and knelt before him and mocked him, saying, "Hail, King of the Jews!" ³⁰They spat on him, and took the reed and struck him on the head. ³¹After mocking him, they stripped him of the robe and put his own clothes on him. Then they led him away to crucify him.*

JOHN 19:1–5 *¹Then Pilate took Jesus and had him flogged. ²And the soldiers wove a crown of thorns and put it on his head, and they dressed him in a purple robe. ³They kept coming up to him, saying, "Hail, King of the Jews!" and striking him on the face. ⁴Pilate went out again and said to them, "Look, I am bringing him out to you to let you know that I find no case against him." ⁵So Jesus came out, wearing the crown of thorns and the purple robe. Pilate said to them, "Here is the man!"*

The humiliation Jesus experienced during his passion was one of the deepest dimensions of his suffering. The soldiers mocked Jesus as a king: for royal garments, they placed a soldier's robe on his battered body; for a diadem, they pressed a crown of spiked thorns into his skull; for a scepter, they put a reed in his right hand. (Matt 27:28–29; John 19:2). Their derision continued as they knelt before him in mock homage and hailed him as king of the Jews, while spitting on him and striking his head (Matt 27:30; John 19:3).

Irony pervades the scene because what the soldiers say and do bespeaks a profound truth about the kingly dignity of Jesus, but on a level they cannot comprehend. Jesus is worthy of their homage, but the true nature of his kingship is hidden in lowly humility and suffering. Stressing the kingship of Christ precisely when he is stripped, scourged, ridiculed, and nailed to a cross proclaims that the passion and death of Jesus is truly his enthronement as king. On the cross Jesus inaugurates his kingdom, conquering sin and death, establishing his reign with non-violent love and justice. When asked by Pilate if he is a king, the most that Jesus would offer is that his kingdom is not of this world. Jesus is king of all people, reigning in a manner totally different from all earthly expectations.

Pilate brought Jesus outside, held him up on display, and told the crowd to look at him: "Here is the man!" (John 19:5). Here is Jesus, broken in body, shaking in torturous pain, looked upon with scorn and derision, laughed at and derided, bloody and beaten, stripped of dignity and identity. This is the history of our cruel humanity, what we do to one another, sin incarnated in Christ's body and blood. This is what hatred, arrogance, and violence does to human beings. Looking at Jesus forces us to look and see what we do to the least of our brothers and sisters.

In the third sorrowful mystery, we contemplate the crown of thorns as the symbol of the kingdom Christ came to bring. It is a kingdom inherited by the meek and merciful. The crown of thorns reminds us that the world's strongest power chose to use his authority at the service of the weakest. The broken man crowned with thorns, the one who mounted a course and painful throne, is truly the King of kings.

Reflection and discussion

• Why is the crown of thorns an apt symbol of the type of kingdom Christ came to bring?

• In what ways is the reign of Christ totally different from the kingdoms of this world? How does Christ exercise his royal power?

• How is Pilate's proclamation, "Here is the man," a challenge to contemplate the sufferings of humanity?

Prayer

King of kings, you were ridiculed and beaten, suffering physical pain and the cruelest humiliation. In your broken body, you displayed the bitter suffering of humanity and the merciful love of God. Give me the courage to stand with you, witnessing always to the truth of love.

So they took Jesus; and carrying the cross by himself, he went out to what is called The Place of the Skull, which in Hebrew is called Golgotha. John 19:17

The Carrying of the Cross

LUKE 23:26–31 *²⁶As they led him away, they seized a man, Simon of Cyrene, who was coming from the country, and they laid the cross on him, and made him carry it behind Jesus. ²⁷A great number of the people followed him, and among them were women who were beating their breasts and wailing for him. ²⁸But Jesus turned to them and said, "Daughters of Jerusalem, do not weep for me, but weep for yourselves and for your children. ²⁹For the days are surely coming when they will say, 'Blessed are the barren, and the wombs that never bore, and the breasts that never nursed.' ³⁰Then they will begin to say to the mountains, 'Fall on us'; and to the hills, 'Cover us.' ³¹For if they do this when the wood is green, what will happen when it is dry?"*

JOHN 19:16–18 *¹⁶Then he handed him over to them to be crucified. So they took Jesus; ¹⁷and carrying the cross by himself, he went out to what is called The Place of the Skull, which in Hebrew is called Golgotha. ¹⁸There they crucified him, and with him two others, one on either side, with Jesus between them.*

The fourth sorrowful mystery, the way of the cross, in one form or another, is everyone's way. That's why Jesus, loving us to the end, took the way of the cross ahead of us. When we experience the inevitable burdens, afflictions, sufferings, and losses of life, we can look to Jesus who walked the Via Dolorosa, the sorrowful journey, ahead of us. Before Jesus took the cross upon his back, he had already taught his followers the clearest definition of discipleship: "If any want to become my followers, let them deny themselves and take up their cross daily and follow me" (Luke 9:23). Taking up the cross each day is the way to be a disciple of Jesus Christ.

As Jesus was carrying his cross to the place of his execution, Simon of Cyrene, a previously unknown passerby who was coming into the city from the countryside, was coerced by the soldiers to carry the cross. Jesus was probably already so physically weak from his torturous scourging that his executioners feared his death before his crucifixion. What must have seemed to Simon at first a terrible indignity, carrying the cross of a condemned man, became his moment of glory. Taking up the cross and carrying it behind Jesus is the definition Jesus had given of discipleship. In that moment, when the chosen disciples had fled and were nowhere to be found, the unknown Simon of Cyrene came to represent true discipleship for all who would hear the gospel of Christ's passion.

Roman crucifixions took place outside the walls of the city, but usually along a major road leading from the city so that crowds could witness what happened when someone dared to revolt against the authority of the empire. The way of the cross led from the place of Jesus' trial, through the city gates, to Golgotha, the eerie Place of the Skull. Earlier that same week Jesus had royally entered Jerusalem, with the whole multitude of disciples praising God and welcoming "the king who comes in the name of the Lord" (Luke 19:37–38). Now Jesus exits the city, staggering and humiliated. Some of the multitude were weeping and mourning his suffering; others were shouting mocking insults.

As Jesus makes his way to his execution, Jesus demonstrates his concern for the people of the city: "Daughters of Jerusalem, do not weep for me, but weep for yourselves and for your children" (Luke 23:28). He is grieved not for his own suffering and impending death, but for the horrible suffering that would soon come upon the city of Jerusalem. Because they would reject the kingdom Jesus came to bring and chose the path of insurrection over the way of non-violence, the road of rebellion over the way of the cross, their city would soon be destroyed by the armies of Rome. Rather than focus on the anguish of Jesus alone, he himself recommends that we ponder his cross in solidarity with our own burdens and with suffering people everywhere. The agony, the scourging, the crown of thorns, the cross and the nails, all have their equivalents in the lives of God's people.

Reflection and discussion

• How does Jesus demonstrate his solidarity with suffering humanity through the way of his cross?

• In what way has Simon of Cyrene become an image of true discipleship? How might he have been changed forever on that fateful day?

• When have I found it difficult to carry my cross? Who helped me carry my cross or made its burden easier?

Prayer

Suffering Lord, your sorrowful journey is the way of all people as we experience life's inevitable pain. As I take up the cross and follow in your footsteps, teach me to walk in solidarity with your suffering people everywhere.

They crucified Jesus there with the criminals, one on his right and one on his left. Then Jesus said, "Father, forgive them; for they do not know what they are doing." Luke 23:33–34

The Crucifixion and Death of Jesus

LUKE 23:32–43 ³²*Two others also, who were criminals, were led away to be put to death with him.* ³³*When they came to the place that is called The Skull, they crucified Jesus there with the criminals, one on his right and one on his left.* ³⁴*Then Jesus said, "Father, forgive them; for they do not know what they are doing." And they cast lots to divide his clothing.* ³⁵*And the people stood by, watching; but the leaders scoffed at him, saying, "He saved others; let him save himself if he is the Messiah of God, his chosen one!"* ³⁶*The soldiers also mocked him, coming up and offering him sour wine,* ³⁷*and saying, "If you are the King of the Jews, save yourself!"* ³⁸*There was also an inscription over him, "This is the King of the Jews."*

³⁹*One of the criminals who were hanged there kept deriding him and saying, "Are you not the Messiah? Save yourself and us!"* ⁴⁰*But the other rebuked him, saying, "Do you not fear God, since you are under the same sentence of condemnation?* ⁴¹*And we indeed have been condemned justly, for we are getting what we deserve for our deeds, but this man has done nothing wrong."* ⁴²*Then he said, "Jesus, remember me when you come into your kingdom."* ⁴³*He replied, "Truly I tell you, today you will be with me in Paradise."*

JOHN 19:25–30 *²⁵Meanwhile, standing near the cross of Jesus were his mother, and his mother's sister, Mary the wife of Clopas, and Mary Magdalene. ²⁶When Jesus saw his mother and the disciple whom he loved standing beside her, he said to his mother, "Woman, here is your son." ²⁷Then he said to the disciple, "Here is your mother." And from that hour the disciple took her into his own home.*

²⁸After this, when Jesus knew that all was now finished, he said (in order to fulfill the scripture), "I am thirsty." ²⁹A jar full of sour wine was standing there. So they put a sponge full of the wine on a branch of hyssop and held it to his mouth. ³⁰When Jesus had received the wine, he said, "It is finished." Then he bowed his head and gave up his spirit.

T he final sorrowful mystery, the crucifixion and death of Jesus, is the climax of his passion and threshold to his glory. The gospels do not describe the crucifixion in detail because that most brutal of human tortures was well known in ancient times. Instead they describe the nobility of Christ's death. This is life lived with love to the end, even unto death on a cross. The cross is both tragic and triumphant. In the ancient Roman world, parents who passed by the road lined with crosses would say to their children, "See, that's what happens to people when they live a bad life." But the life and death of Jesus transformed the cross from a hated instrument of punishment to a glorious sign of saving love. Now Christian parents who point out the cross to their children say, "See, that's how much God was willing to do for you to show his love."

A God who remained isolated from human suffering, majestically insulated in his heaven, would not be a convincing or reliable God in our suffering world. Instead God entered our world of flesh and blood, tears and death. The cross is our most powerful reminder that God is with us even in pain and tragedy and seemingly hopeless situations. In every moment of suffering and death, we can find our God. He has borne and transformed our humanity and our mortality, and so we are saved now, even from the clutch, the threat, and the dread of death. In looking at the Crucified One we see the power of life and of love. In the crucifixion of his Son, God's saving love was expressed most conclusively.

Even to the end, Jesus continued to express his saving mission and carry out his Father's redemptive plan. Though he had been falsely accused, scornfully mocked, and brutally battered, he responded with love by showing mercy even to his executioners: "Father, forgive them; for they do not know what they are doing" (Luke 23:34). Hanging from the cross, Jesus most fully embodies his teaching to love even those who have offended and wronged us: "Love your enemies, do good to those who hate you, bless those who curse you, pray for those who abuse you" (Luke 6:27–28). And in his final act before he died, Jesus grants salvation to the repentant criminal dying on the cross beside him: "Truly I tell you, today you will be with me in Paradise" (Luke 23:43). Because of the mercy he received, the crucified criminal is the first to recognize that the cross is the world's clearest sign of God's glorious love.

For all those who loved and followed Jesus, the crucifixion was a day of tragic horror. Yet no grief could compare to that of his mother. The sword that Simeon had prophesied would pierce Mary's soul (Luke 2:35) now struck its deepest wound. How Mary could hold and ponder this too in her heart can be understood only by parents who have suffered the deaths of their children. The child whose birth was announced to Mary by God's angel and for whom the angels sang at his birth in Bethlehem now died in agony while the heavens remained incomprehensively silent. But loving to the end, Jesus entrusted his mother to his beloved disciple and the disciple to his mother (John 19:26 27). From that moment, Mary gained the filial care of a new son and all disciples gained a mother who would be tender and faithful now and at the hour of our death. She would continue to treasure the mysteries of her Son's life in her heart and ponder with his disciples the meaning of his redeeming death.

Reflection and discussion

• How is the sign of the cross transformed by the divine person who was crucified and died upon it?

• How could Jesus forgive his accusers, torturers, and executioners? How does his mercy help me to forgive others?

• How do the sorrowful mysteries of Christ's passion make God more convincing and credible to a suffering world?

• In what way do I experience Mary's maternal care? How does she help me contemplate the mysteries of Christ's life and death?

Prayer

Crucified Savior, you entered most fully into the experience of grief and suffering, and in your dying agony you showed me the fullness of mercy and love. Teach me how to be fully human, graced, and holy in all the circumstances of life, now and at the hour of my death.

SUGGESTIONS FOR FACILITATORS, GROUP SESSION 5

1. Welcome group members and ask if anyone has any questions, announcements, or requests.

2. You may want to pray this prayer as a group:

Saving Lord, the sorrowful mysteries of the rosary express the suffering of your passion and your passionate love for us. Your agony in the garden, scourging at the pillar, crowning with thorns, carrying the cross, and crucifixion reveals the totality of your love for us in our suffering world. In you our sin finds forgiveness, our brokenness is made whole, and our spiritual illness is healed. Help us to find hope in our suffering and follow the way of the cross to the life you have promised us.

3. Ask one or more of the following questions:

   • What insight from the passion of Christ most inspired you from this week's study?
   • What new understanding of the sorrowful mysteries stands out for you this week?

4. Discuss lessons 19 through 24. Choose one or more of the questions for reflection and discussion from each lesson to talk over as a group.

5. Ask the group members to name one thing they have most appreciated about the way the group has worked during this Bible study. Ask group members to discuss any changes they might suggest in the way the group functions in future studies.

6. Invite group members to complete lessons 25 through 30 on their own during the six days before the next meeting. They should write out their own answers to the questions as preparation for next week's session.

7. Ask the group how this study is affecting the way they meditate on the mysteries of Christ.

8. Conclude by praying aloud together the prayer at the end of one of the lessons discussed. You may want to end the prayer by asking members to voice prayers of thanksgiving.

He has remembered his steadfast love and faithfulness to the house of Israel. All the ends of the earth have seen the victory of our God. Ps 98:3

The Glorious Mysteries

PSALM 98:1–6

¹*O sing to the Lord a new song,*
  for he has done marvelous things.
His right hand and his holy arm
  have gained him victory.
²*The Lord has made known his victory;*
  he has revealed his vindication in the sight of the nations.
³*He has remembered his steadfast love and faithfulness*
  to the house of Israel.
All the ends of the earth have seen
  the victory of our God.

⁴*Make a joyful noise to the Lord, all the earth;*
  break forth into joyous song and sing praises.
⁵*Sing praises to the Lord with the lyre,*
  with the lyre and the sound of melody.
⁶*With trumpets and the sound of the horn*
  make a joyful noise before the King, the Lord.

JOHN 16:21–24 ²¹*When a woman is in labor, she has pain, because her hour has come. But when her child is born, she no longer remembers the anguish*

because of the joy of having brought a human being into the world. ²²So you have pain now; but I will see you again, and your hearts will rejoice, and no one will take your joy from you. ²³On that day you will ask nothing of me. Very truly, I tell you, if you ask anything of the Father in my name, he will give it to you. ²⁴Until now you have not asked for anything in my name. Ask and you will receive, so that your joy may be complete.

JOHN 17:1–5 ¹*After Jesus had spoken these words, he looked up to heaven and said, "Father, the hour has come; glorify your Son so that the Son may glorify you, ²since you have given him authority over all people, to give eternal life to all whom you have given him. ³And this is eternal life, that they may know you, the only true God, and Jesus Christ whom you have sent. ⁴I glorified you on earth by finishing the work that you gave me to do. ⁵So now, Father, glorify me in your own presence with the glory that I had in your presence before the world existed."*

The five glorious mysteries of the rosary invite us to look beyond the darkness of Christ's sorrowful passion to contemplate the glory of his risen life. The resurrection of Jesus, the first glorious mystery, is the source of all the others. It was the transforming event that turned dejected disciples into hopeful bearers of good news. The second mystery, the ascension of Jesus, expresses the glorious presence of Christ, reigning in heaven and interceding for us always. The coming of the Holy Spirit, the third mystery, transforms us so that we personally experience the risen glory of Christ and become children of God. The final two mysteries present Mary as the completion of what God is doing within us. Filled with God's Spirit, she shares Christ's glory fully in the splendors of heaven. She continues to be the glorious mother of Christ and mother of his disciples, the queen of heaven and royal mother of Christ's church on earth.

Psalm 98 calls on all God's people to give praise to God in song for the "victory" God has won because of his "steadfast love and faithfulness." God's triumph for the sake of his people was manifested to "all the ends of the earth" (Ps 98:1–3). The lyre, trumpet, and horn accompany the joyous song and praises creating "a joyful noise to the Lord" by all the earth (Ps 98:4–6). The psalm must have been sung throughout Israel's history to celebrate the manifestations of God's power and victory in the midst of his people. But there is no greater and more glorious victory of God than the resurrection of Christ.

The psalm has been sung through the ages by the church to proclaim God's triumph over sin, evil, death, and all that impedes the glorious coming of God's kingdom. This is the "new song" that celebrates the "marvelous things" that God has done in the glorious mysteries of Christ's victory.

In his final discourse, Jesus used the experience of a woman in childbirth to explain how the disciples' sorrow will turn into joy (John 16:21–22). Before birth she experienced pain and anguish because she has come to her "hour." After the child's birth, the sorrow is seen only as the means to experience a joy that cannot be taken away. At the miracle of Cana, when the mother of Jesus initiated his saving work, the "hour" had not yet come. Yet that first sign was the first of many that would reveal his glory (John 2:4, 11). The sorrowful "hour" of Christ's passion would be the final means to reveal his full glory. With the glorification of Christ and the sending of the Holy Spirit, the new relationship of the disciples with the Father will enable them to approach him confidently in prayer. As disciples of the risen Lord, we will ask and receive, and our joy will be complete (John 16:23–24).

In meditating on the glorious mysteries, we ponder the completion of the work that the Father had given Christ to do on the earth (John 17:4). The result of that saving work was the gift of "eternal life," the fullness of life that comes with knowing and experiencing God as revealed through Jesus Christ (John 17:2–3). As the Father is glorified through Christ, so Christ is glorified by the Father as he restores his Son to his presence. And from his place in heaven, Christ is present to us through his Spirit and intercedes for us with the Father so that we may experience, like Mary, the completion of God's eternal plan for our salvation.

Reflection and discussion

• Why are these five mysteries called "glorious"?

• In what way are the glorious mysteries the "victory" of God? In what ways do I share in the victory?

• How does the image of the woman in childbirth express the unending joy attained through Christ's glorification? In what way does this image express the experience of Mary?

• What is "eternal life" (John 17:3)? How do I experience eternal life already in this life?

Prayer

Lord Jesus Christ, your cross and resurrection is the means by which we are born anew into eternal life. I sing a new song for the marvelous things you have done as you remembered your steadfast love and faithfulness. Thank you for the gift of salvation and its unending joy.

"Why do you look for the living among the dead? He is not here, but has risen." Luke 24:5

The Resurrection of the Lord

LUKE 24:1–12 *¹But on the first day of the week, at early dawn, they came to the tomb, taking the spices that they had prepared. ²They found the stone rolled away from the tomb, ³but when they went in, they did not find the body. ⁴While they were perplexed about this, suddenly two men in dazzling clothes stood beside them. ⁵The women were terrified and bowed their faces to the ground, but the men said to them, "Why do you look for the living among the dead? He is not here, but has risen. ⁶Remember how he told you, while he was still in Galilee, ⁷that the Son of Man must be handed over to sinners, and be crucified, and on the third day rise again." ⁸Then they remembered his words, ⁹and returning from the tomb, they told all this to the eleven and to all the rest. ¹⁰Now it was Mary Magdalene, Joanna, Mary the mother of James, and the other women with them who told this to the apostles. ¹¹But these words seemed to them an idle tale, and they did not believe them. ¹²But Peter got up and ran to the tomb; stooping and looking in, he saw the linen cloths by themselves; then he went home, amazed at what had happened.*

JOHN 20:11–18 *¹¹But Mary stood weeping outside the tomb. As she wept, she bent over to look into the tomb; ¹²and she saw two angels in white, sitting where the body of Jesus had been lying, one at the head and the other at the feet.*

¹³They said to her, "Woman, why are you weeping?" She said to them, "They have taken away my Lord, and I do not know where they have laid him." ¹⁴When she had said this, she turned around and saw Jesus standing there, but she did not know that it was Jesus. ¹⁵Jesus said to her, "Woman, why are you weeping? Whom are you looking for?" Supposing him to be the gardener, she said to him, "Sir, if you have carried him away, tell me where you have laid him, and I will take him away." ¹⁶Jesus said to her, "Mary!" She turned and said to him in Hebrew, "Rabbouni!" (which means Teacher). ¹⁷Jesus said to her, "Do not hold on to me, because I have not yet ascended to the Father. But go to my brothers and say to them, 'I am ascending to my Father and your Father, to my God and your God.'" ¹⁸Mary Magdalene went and announced to the disciples, "I have seen the Lord"; and she told them that he had said these things to her.

The darkness and seeming finality of Jesus' death and burial in the tomb is shattered by the marvelous reality of Christ's resurrection. The women came to the tomb at dawn on the first day of the week, the beginning of God's new creation. Finding the tomb empty, they heard the proclamation of the angels that Jesus is risen. Because of the resurrection, the life of Jesus is not tragedy, ending in death; it is gospel—good news to be spread throughout all the earth. The first glorious mystery is the new and transformed life of Jesus that creates the Christian faith; it is the spark that set the disciples on fire and changed them into a jubilant community.

The Son of God descended into our fallen humanity in order to raise us up to share in his divinity. In his incarnation and birth, he lowered himself into our world to become flesh and dwell with us. In his public life, he continued to descend, journeying deeply into the lives of humanity's outcastes. By meeting them at their lowest points, he healed them, forgave them, delivered them from evil and restored them to life. Jesus descended most completely into our suffering and sinfulness on the cross. And meeting us there, at the bottom of humanity, Jesus transforms our human nature and lifts it up with him in resurrection.

The gospel accounts build up evidence for the real and bodily nature of the resurrection. When Peter looked into the tomb, "he saw the linen cloths by themselves" (Luke 24:12). If anyone had wanted to remove the body of Jesus, they would not have left the grave clothes behind. They would have certainly carried the body away in its shroud. The stress on the empty tomb and the absence of Christ's body expresses the fact that the resurrection is something that happened to Jesus, and is not just a subjective experience in the minds of his disciples. The disciples were changed because they discovered that the body of Jesus had been transformed through resurrection.

Jesus was the first in the human family to be raised and glorified. We see in him what God has promised for our destiny—resurrection from the dead and the fullness of life forever. Though dead and physically corrupted, we will be recalled to life by a new act of creation by God on the last day. Yet, the resurrection of Jesus is not just good news for our future. In his resurrection the future has already invaded the present. Death can already be mocked as a defeated enemy: "Where, O death, is your sting?" (1 Cor 15:55). Christ's resurrection offers us a power for living to overcome even the most difficult obstacles and a purpose for living that assures us that what we do is not in vain.

When Mary Magdalene proclaims, "I have seen the Lord" (John 20:18), she is referring to an experience far deeper and more real than simply a visual sighting. The experience is one of loving recognition, a deeply personal encounter with Christ. She has moved from the darkness to the light of faith. She wants to hold on to Jesus, but Jesus says, "Do not hold on to me, because I have not yet ascended to the Father" (John 20:17). With his ascension and the sending of the Holy Spirit, Jesus would be intimately present to her and to all who seek him.

Reflection and discussion

• In what ways do the gospels indicate that Christ's resurrection is a real and objective experience? What evidence do I need?

• What emotions do I imagine Mary Magdalene and the other women must have experienced at the empty tomb of Jesus?

• What is the lowest point in my life to which Jesus has descended? How have I been raised with him to share in his new life?

• In what way does the resurrection of Jesus give hope for my future and purpose for my living?

Prayer

Risen Lord of Life, you are the light that shines in the world's darkness, the beginning of God's new creation. Lead me as I discover, like your first disciples, the wonderful news of your risen life, and help me to trust that life, mercy, and love are stronger than death, hate, and evil.

"Men of Galilee, why do you stand looking up toward heaven? This Jesus, who has been taken up from you into heaven, will come in the same way as you saw him go into heaven." Acts 1:11

The Ascension into Heaven

ACTS 1:1–14 *¹In the first book, Theophilus, I wrote about all that Jesus did and taught from the beginning ²until the day when he was taken up to heaven, after giving instructions through the Holy Spirit to the apostles whom he had chosen. ³After his suffering he presented himself alive to them by many convincing proofs, appearing to them during forty days and speaking about the kingdom of God. ⁴While staying with them, he ordered them not to leave Jerusalem, but to wait there for the promise of the Father. "This," he said, "is what you have heard from me; ⁵for John baptized with water, but you will be baptized with the Holy Spirit not many days from now."*

⁶So when they had come together, they asked him, "Lord, is this the time when you will restore the kingdom to Israel?" ⁷He replied, "It is not for you to know the times or periods that the Father has set by his own authority. ⁸But you will receive power when the Holy Spirit has come upon you; and you will be my witnesses in Jerusalem, in all Judea and Samaria, and to the ends of the earth." ⁹When he had said this, as they were watching, he was lifted up, and a cloud took him out of their sight. ¹⁰While he was going and they were gazing up toward heaven, suddenly two men in white robes stood by them. ¹¹They said, "Men of Galilee, why do you stand looking up toward heaven? This Jesus, who has been taken up from you into heaven, will come in the same way as you saw him go into heaven."

¹² *Then they returned to Jerusalem from the mount called Olivet, which is near Jerusalem, a sabbath day's journey away.* ¹³ *When they had entered the city, they went to the room upstairs where they were staying, Peter, and John, and James, and Andrew, Philip and Thomas, Bartholomew and Matthew, James son of Alphaeus, and Simon the Zealot, and Judas son of James.* ¹⁴ *All these were constantly devoting themselves to prayer, together with certain women, including Mary the mother of Jesus, as well as his brothers.*

The second glorious mystery invites us to reflect on the final passage of the risen Jesus to the glory of God. Luke, the writer of the Acts of the Apostles, uses a spatial image to express the withdrawing of the bodily presence of Jesus from the community of his disciples: "He was lifted up, and a cloud took him out of their sight" (verse 9). From now on, Jesus will be present with his disciples in a new way. As the crucified and risen Lord in his heavenly existence, Jesus will intercede on our behalf and yet also remain with us forever in the power of the Holy Spirit.

Luke narrates the ascension of Jesus at the beginning of his story of the church. After learning about God's kingdom from Jesus throughout his earthly ministry, the disciples now ask if the time has come for Jesus to complete the coming of his kingdom (verse 6). This future kingdom would extend God's reign over all the earth, gathering all people to worship the one God. Jesus tells his disciples that they will not know the times the Father has set to bring the fullness of the kingdom, but that they would have an essential role in its preparation. They will carry on his ministry until he returns, undertaking a worldwide evangelizing mission "to the ends of the earth" (verse 8), through the power of the Holy Spirit.

The question asked by the two men in white robes, "Why do you stand looking up toward heaven?" is very similar to the question asked by the same two dazzling figures in Luke's account of the resurrection, "Why do you look for the living one among the dead?" (Luke 24:5). Each question implies that the presence of Jesus has been transformed and that this new reality implies a new task for his followers. In each scene, the question challenges the hearers to take up their new task, and each question is followed by a proclamation that sets them off on their mission. We cannot find Jesus by searching among the dead or by looking up to heaven. He will return to us, but until then we have a mission to perform.

Between the time of Jesus' ascension to heaven and his return from heaven is the time of the church. In this middle-time, the community of the risen Lord has a job to do, as described in the following chapters of the Acts of the Apostles. Each of us has a role to play as a witness to the good news of Christ as we await his coming in glory and the full completion of his kingdom.

Reflection and discussion

• In what new way is Jesus present with his church after his ascension to heaven?

• Why must the disciples move from "looking up toward heaven" to "the ends of the earth"?0 How does Jesus define my mission until he returns?

Prayer

Risen and Glorious Lord, you have ascended to your Father but you entrusted us with the mission of extending your good news to the ends of the earth. Help me to find places where the truth and love of your gospel have not penetrated so that I can carry out my call to be your witness.

Divided tongues, as of fire, appeared among them, and a tongue rested on each of them. All of them were filled with the Holy Spirit and began to speak in other languages, as the Spirit gave them ability. Acts 2:3–4

The Descent of the Holy Spirit

ACTS 2:1–13 *¹When the day of Pentecost had come, they were all together in one place. ²And suddenly from heaven there came a sound like the rush of a violent wind, and it filled the entire house where they were sitting. ³Divided tongues, as of fire, appeared among them, and a tongue rested on each of them. ⁴All of them were filled with the Holy Spirit and began to speak in other languages, as the Spirit gave them ability.*

⁵Now there were devout Jews from every nation under heaven living in Jerusalem. ⁶And at this sound the crowd gathered and was bewildered, because each one heard them speaking in the native language of each. ⁷Amazed and astonished, they asked, "Are not all these who are speaking Galileans? ⁸And how is it that we hear, each of us, in our own native language? ⁹Parthians, Medes, Elamites, and residents of Mesopotamia, Judea and Cappadocia, Pontus and Asia, ¹⁰Phrygia and Pamphylia, Egypt and the parts of Libya belonging to Cyrene, and visitors from Rome, both Jews and proselytes, ¹¹Cretans and Arabs— in our own languages we hear them speaking about God's deeds of power." ¹²All were amazed and perplexed, saying to one another, "What does this mean?" ¹³But others sneered and said, "They are filled with new wine."

The feast of Pentecost was a Jewish festival during which Jews would come to Jerusalem on pilgrimage to offer the first fruits of the wheat harvest. The feast was celebrated fifty days after the feast of Passover, and recalled the giving of the Torah to Israel at Mount Sinai after their departure from Egypt. The descent of the Holy Spirit, the third glorious mystery, is described by Luke in ways that bring out its connection with God's establishment of Israel as his covenanted people at Mount Sinai. As the covenant was established at Mount Sinai fifty days after the Passover lambs were sacrificed in Egypt, so now the church is established through the power of God's Spirit fifty days after the Lamb of God was sacrificed on the cross. The old covenant constituted the Israelites as the people of God; now the coming of Holy Spirit established the disciples as the church of Jesus Christ. The reconstituted twelve apostles (Judas had already been replaced by Matthias, Acts 1:26) are gathered like the twelve tribes at Sinai. Just as God descended on Mount Sinai in the form of fire, accompanied by the sound of a trumpet blast and thunder (Exod 19:16–19), so now God's Holy Spirit descends in Jerusalem with the astonishing signs of fire and a loud sound like violent winds. As the new Pentecost, the descent of the Holy Spirit makes a new beginning in salvation history, the birth of the church as the universal people of God.

The list of the nationalities of the Jewish pilgrims in Jerusalem (verses 9–11) expresses the future implications of God's gift of the Spirit. The broad sweep of nationalities from East to West foreshadows the universality of the Christian mission. The fact that the international crowd hears the apostles speak in their own language signals the reversal of the curse of the tower of Babel (Gen 11:7–9). Then God had diversified the languages of humanity so that they could not understand one another and scattered them across the earth. Now God's Spirit is overcoming the effects of human sin as the fractured human family is being reunited in Christ's church. The people were amazed and perplexed, and they said to one another, "What does this mean?" (verse 12). The rest of the Acts of the Apostles explains the meaning of Pentecost as it unfolds the story of the Spirit-led mission of the church.

Luke states that "Mary the mother of Jesus" was gathered in the upper room with the apostles "constantly devoting themselves to prayer" in anticipation of the Spirit's coming (Acts 1:14). Mary, who had conceived Christ in her womb by the overshadowing power of the Holy Spirit, now prays that the same Holy Spirit would come upon the gathered apostles. Once the action of

God's Spirit had formed the physical body of Christ within Mary's womb; now that Spirit would form the mystical body of Christ, the Spirit-conceived church. The mother who welcomed the actions of God's Spirit in her life at the Annunciation (Luke 1:35), the mother who watched Jesus beneath the cross as he commended his spirit into the Father's hands (Luke 23:46), and the mother who prayed for the coming of the Spirit upon the apostles, continues to extend her maternal prayers for us, fostering the coming of the Holy Spirit into our lives and into our world today.

Reflection and discussion

• How do the events at Pentecost foreshadow what will enfold in the early history of the church as described throughout the Acts of the Apostles?

• In what ways am I most aware of the Holy Spirit's presence and power? In what new way might God be wanting to act in my life today?

Prayer

Holy Spirit of the living God, draw me more deeply into your divine life. Stir into flame the fire of faith and love that you initiated in me at baptism. Transform me and renew me with your gifts so that I may be an effective witness of Jesus Christ in the world.

When this perishable body puts on imperishability, and this mortal body puts on immortality, then the saying that is written will be fulfilled: "Death has been swallowed up in victory." 1 Cor 15:54

The Assumption of Mary

1 CORINTHIANS 15:12–23, 50–57

¹²*Now if Christ is proclaimed as raised from the dead, how can some of you say there is no resurrection of the dead? ¹³If there is no resurrection of the dead, then Christ has not been raised; ¹⁴and if Christ has not been raised, then our proclamation has been in vain and your faith has been in vain. ¹⁵We are even found to be misrepresenting God, because we testified of God that he raised Christ—whom he did not raise if it is true that the dead are not raised. ¹⁶For if the dead are not raised, then Christ has not been raised. ¹⁷If Christ has not been raised, your faith is futile and you are still in your sins. ¹⁸Then those also who have died in Christ have perished. ¹⁹If for this life only we have hoped in Christ, we are of all people most to be pitied.*

²⁰But in fact Christ has been raised from the dead, the first fruits of those who have died. ²¹For since death came through a human being, the resurrection of the dead has also come through a human being; ²²for as all die in Adam, so all will be made alive in Christ. ²³But each in his own order: Christ the first fruits, then at his coming those who belong to Christ.

⁵⁰What I am saying, brothers and sisters, is this: flesh and blood cannot inherit the kingdom of God, nor does the perishable inherit the imperishable. ⁵¹Listen, I will tell you a mystery! We will not all die, but we will all be changed, ⁵²in a moment, in the twinkling of an eye, at the last trumpet. For the trumpet will sound, and the dead will be raised imperishable, and we will be

changed. [53] *For this perishable body must put on imperishability, and this mortal body must put on immortality.* [54] *When this perishable body puts on imperishability, and this mortal body puts on immortality, then the saying that is written will be fulfilled:*
  "Death has been swallowed up in victory."
  [55] *"Where, O death, is your victory?*
       Where, O death, is your sting?"
[56] *The sting of death is sin, and the power of sin is the law.* [57] *But thanks be to God, who gives us the victory through our Lord Jesus Christ.*

The fourth glorious mystery, the Assumption of Mary, expresses the church's ancient belief that the mother of Christ was taken to heaven when her earthly life was finished. Rather than experience bodily corruption and await the resurrection of the body, Mary experienced the glorified life, body and soul, immediately after her death. This mystery represents what awaits all of us who trust in God's power to give new life to our mortal bodies. As the mother of all Christ's disciples, Mary is the anticipation and the supreme realization of our final glory. She is the icon and model of what God will do for those who wait in faith, hope, and love.

In writing about the resurrection, Paul insists that the whole human person, created by God, will be given a new, transformed bodily life through the resurrection of the dead. By calling the risen Christ the "first fruits of those who have died," Paul indicates that Christ's resurrection is an anticipatory promise of the general resurrection of all believers (verses 20–23). We live now in the interval between Christ's resurrection and the day of Christ's coming when the dead will be raised to life. But because of Christ's resurrection, the future age has already burst into the present age. The time of forgiveness and victory over sin and death, foretold by the ancient prophets and sages of Israel, has already come upon the earth. What happened when Christ rose from the tomb has made the world a different kind of place, and has given us the possibility of becoming a different kind of people.

The resurrection of the dead is not just the resuscitation of physical corpses. Paul explains that the resurrection entails transformation of the body into a new and glorious state: "For this perishable body must put on imperishability, and this mortal body must put on immortality" (verse 53). When Christ rose from the dead, he did not leave his human nature behind. Rather, in his resurrection and ascension, he lifted our human nature up to victory over death, its greatest enemy, and he has raised our human nature right up into the presence of God forever. This is the ultimate victory he has in mind for us. He intends to have us join him where he is, in the glorious presence of God forever.

Since Mary was the first and preeminent disciple, the first to hear God's word and accept it, she was also the first to experience the blessings of following Christ, especially the victory over death. She was the first to receive the new, transformed life that is promised to all the faithful ones. She embodies the final destiny of all who are redeemed in Christ and she expresses the final victory of God's grace which saves the whole person, body and soul. Mary shines forth on earth, until the day of the Lord comes, as a sign of sure hope for the pilgrim people of God. She is the first flowering of the church as it will be perfected in the world to come.

Reflection and discussion

• In what way is the Assumption of Mary an icon and model of what God has promised for his whole church?

• What offers me the greatest confidence that God will raise me and those I love to eternal life on the last day?

• In what way do the words of Paul take away the "sting" (verses 55) of death for me?

• In what ways is Mary the first and preeminent disciple?

• What does the glorified life of Mary in heaven tell me about the dignity of our human nature and the power of God's grace?

Prayer

Lord Jesus Christ, you have destroyed the powers of death and given me confidence in the future. Without you I am trapped in sin and destined for eternal death. Because of you death's fate is sealed and I can live in joyful hope.

The king rose to meet her, and bowed down to her; then he sat on his throne, and had a throne brought for the king's mother, and she sat on his right. 1 Kings 2:19

The Coronation of Mary as Queen of Heaven

1 KINGS 2:16–20 ¹⁶*"And now I have one request to make of you; do not refuse me." [The king's mother, Bathsheba] said to him, "Go on." ¹⁷He said, "Please ask King Solomon—he will not refuse you—to give me Abishag the Shunammite as my wife." ¹⁸Bathsheba said, "Very well; I will speak to the king on your behalf." ¹⁹So Bathsheba went to King Solomon, to speak to him on behalf of Adonijah. The king rose to meet her, and bowed down to her; then he sat on his throne, and had a throne brought for the king's mother, and she sat on his right. ²⁰Then she said, "I have one small request to make of you; do not refuse me." And the king said to her, "Make your request, my mother; for I will not refuse you."*

REVELATION 12:1–8, 13–17 ¹*A great portent appeared in heaven: a woman clothed with the sun, with the moon under her feet, and on her head a crown of twelve stars. ²She was pregnant and was crying out in birthpangs, in the agony of giving birth. ³Then another portent appeared in heaven: a great red dragon, with seven heads and ten horns, and seven diadems on his heads. ⁴His tail swept down a third of the stars of heaven and threw them to the earth. Then the dragon stood before the woman who was about to bear a child, so that he might devour her child as soon as it was born. ⁵And she gave birth to a son, a* *male child, who is to rule all the nations with a rod of iron. But her child was snatched away and taken to God and to his throne; ⁶and the woman fled into the wilderness, where she has a place prepared by God, so that there she can be nourished for one thousand two hundred sixty days. ⁷And war broke out in heaven; Michael and his angels fought against the dragon. The dragon and his angels fought back, ⁸but they were defeated, and there was no longer any place for them in heaven.*

¹³So when the dragon saw that he had been thrown down to the earth, he pursued the woman who had given birth to the male child. ¹⁴But the woman was given the two wings of the great eagle, so that she could fly from the serpent into the wilderness, to her place where she is nourished for a time, and times, and half a time. ¹⁵Then from his mouth the serpent poured water like a river after the woman, to sweep her away with the flood. ¹⁶But the earth came to the help of the woman; it opened its mouth and swallowed the river that the dragon had poured from his mouth. ¹⁷Then the dragon was angry with the woman, and went off to make war on the rest of her children, those who keep the commandments of God and hold the testimony of Jesus.

Meditating on the fifth glorious mystery, the crowning of Mary as queen of heaven, reminds us that we too are called to live in the reign of God as heirs of the kingdom that has no end. We are "a chosen race, a royal priesthood, a holy nation, God's own people" (1 Pet 2:9). Mary's royal status is rooted in her role as the mother of God's Messiah, the King of kings, and therefore queen mother of all his disciples. Our tribute to Mary's queenship is also a remembrance of our membership in the royal family of Christ.

In ancient Israel, the woman who sat on the throne next to the king was his mother. Most monarchs in that ancient world had multiple wives, but it was the king's mother who exercised the royal status as queen. She was usually introduced by name whenever a new king came to the throne in Jerusalem, and she sat on a throne to the king's right and wore a royal crown (1 Kgs 2:19; Jer 13:18). The petition of Queen Bathsheba made to her son Solomon demonstrates the role of the queen mother as an advocate for the people, presenting their requests to her royal son. Knowing that the king always listens to the intercession of the queen mother, the people confidently made their requests to her: "Please ask King Solomon—he will not refuse you" (1 Kgs 2:17).

As the Messiah, Jesus is the new Son of David, who fulfilled all God's promises to King David. His kingdom is not of this world, yet his reign is universal and everlasting. The title bestowed on Mary by Elizabeth, "mother of my Lord" (Luke 1:43), is a royal accolade heard in the courts of Jerusalem and other royal cities of the ancient world. As mother of Jesus, she is the queen of Christ's heavenly reign. As mother of his church, Mary lovingly presents our needs before Christ's throne and so serves the kingdom by leading people closer to her Son. With her maternal love, she is devoted totally to our salvation.

The identity of the royal woman of Revelation, clothed with the sun and wearing a crown of twelve stars, is found in the identity of her Son to whom she gave birth (Rev 12:1–2, 5). He is the long-awaited Messiah, destined "to rule the nations" from his place at the throne of God. The feminine image describes the church in ultimate victory. But it also describes the embodiment of the church in Mary, the eschatological icon of the church, a prototype already enjoying the glory that the church will eventually share. The glorified feminine body of Mary has joined the glorified masculine body of Jesus in the eternal kingdom of heaven.

The glorious Christ said to his church, "Be faithful until death, and I will give you the crown of life" (Rev 2:10). Mary's faith began with a decision in Nazareth and entailed a lifetime of continual choices, changes, suffering, and growth. The maiden of Nazareth is now, by God's grace at work within her, our holy queen, the mother of mercy. From her place in heaven, she guides us with her maternal care as we meditate on the mysteries of the rosary so that we can become more like him and share in the glorious destiny he has planned for our eternity.

Reflection and discussion

• In what way is Christ a king and Mary a queen, though not of this world?

• In what way is the woman of Revelation 12 an image of the church in glory?

• What is the goal God has in mind for me for all eternity? How does mindfulness of that goal alter my daily life?

• Why does the rosary lead our meditation on Christ's life through the mind and heart of Mary? How has this study led me to a new intimacy with her?

Prayer

Son of God and Son of Mary, as we pray for the coming of your kingdom, help us do the work you began among us. Inspire us to works of justice, compassion, and forgiveness until you come in glory to crown all our efforts with your blessings.

SUGGESTIONS FOR FACILITATORS, GROUP SESSION 6

1. Welcome group members and make any final announcements or requests.

2. You may want to pray this prayer as a group:

King of kings and Lord of lords, the glorious mysteries of the rosary invite us to reflect on your risen and glorious life and on the fullness of life you want to share with us forever. The resurrection, the ascension, and the descent of the Holy Spirit express for us the divine life you want to bestow upon our humanity. The assumption and coronation of Mary in heaven offer us images of the eternal glory you desire for our eternity. Deepen the hope you have given us through the prayers of Mary, the mother of your church both on earth and in heaven.

3. Ask one or more of the following questions:
   • In what way has this study challenged you the most?
   • How has this study deepened your experience of praying the rosary?

4. Discuss lessons 25 through 30. Choose one or more of the questions for reflection and discussion from each lesson to discuss as a group.

5. Ask the group if they would like to study another book in the Threshold Bible Study series. Discuss the topic and dates, and make a decision among those interested. Ask the group members to suggest people they would like to invite to participate in the next study series.

6. Ask the group to discuss the insights that stand out most from this study over the past six weeks and how praying the mysteries of the rosary will hold a richer meaning from now on.

7. Conclude by praying aloud the following prayer or another of your own choosing:

Holy Spirit of God, you inspired the sacred writers of the Bible and you have guided our study during these weeks. Continue to deepen our love for the word of God in the holy Scriptures and draw us as disciples to the fullness of life you promise us through our meditation on the mysteries of the rosary. Sanctify us with the sacrificial love of Christ so that we may offer that love to those we meet. Bless us now and always with the fire of your love.